MW00807567

FANGORIA's
BEST HORROR FILMS

Edited by
ANTHONY TIMPONE

Crescent Books
New York • Avenel, New Jersey

Introduction and Compilation
Copyright © 1994 by Starlog Communications International, Inc.
Fangoria is a trademark of Starlog Communications International, Inc.
All rights reserved.

First published in 1994 by Crescent Books,
distributed by Outlet Book Company, Inc.,
a Random House Company,
40 Engelhard Avenue
Avenel, New Jersey 07001

Designed by Paul Rodriguez and Rebecca Tachna/R Studio T

Manufactured in the United States

Library of Congress Cataloging-in-Publication Data
Fangoria's best horror films / edited by Anthony Timpone.
        p.   cm.
        ISBN 0-517-10013-4 : $14.99
1. Horror films—United States—History and criticism.
   I. Timpone, Anthony. II. Title: Best horror films.
        PN1995.9.H6F33   1994
     791.43'616—dc20   93-46362
                                    CIP

8 7 6 5 4 3 2 1

CONTENTS

HORROR HIT PARADE

© Orion

Welcome to the horror hit parade. In these blood-soaked pages, you will delve into the world of dark entertainment, as reported by the most popular horror journal to ever stalk a newsstand, FANGORIA magazine. Come with us as we tour the chilly crypts of Castle Dracula, the dreaded ghetto haunts of Candyman, the deserted killing fields of the Living Dead, the creepy corridors of the Addams family mansion and the intergalactic hunting ground of the unstoppable Aliens.

As the slasher films of the early '80s breathed their last gasp in the '90s (witness the highly-touted though dubious deaths of both Freddy Krueger and Jason Voorhees in their "Final" films *Freddy's Dead* and *Jason Goes to Hell*), Hollywood began to exploit new avenues of screen terror. *Misery* and *The Silence of the Lambs* successfully mixed elements of Grand Guignol shocks with psychological suspense, winning kudos from the kinds of critics who wouldn't be caught dead at a splatter film. When these films went on to win major Academy Awards honors (including Best Picture for *Silence*), many—including the filmmakers themselves—refused to admit that their films were horror, thus denying the genre the legitimacy that it deserved. But the box-office message was still clear: People enjoy being scared in the safe confines of a darkened movie theater.

While Hollywood continued to exploit the "monster next door" formula of *Fatal Attraction* with such cookie-cutter films as *Sleeping With the Enemy*, *Unlawful Entry*, *The Hand That Rocks the Cradle* and *Single White Female*, the '90s also began embracing the Gothic tradition once again. *Darkman* (a stylized mix of *Phantom of the Opera*, comic-book heroics and mad-scientist mayhem) and *Bram Stoker's Dracula* ushered in a return to the thrills of the Universal and Hammer monster series.

Speaking of monsters, the new generation of horror "heroes" continued to be the fiends behind the masks. Fans and cults took to lionizing supernatural screen stars Robert ("Freddy") Englund, Kane ("Jason") Hodder, Doug ("Pinhead") Bradley and the various *Halloween* actors. These stars strive to follow in the footsteps of the legendary Vincent Price, who reminisced about his amazing cinematic legacy at one of FANGORIA's packed horror conventions. Each of these terror thespians openly share their film experiences in these pages, and you'll learn that they're not such a bad bunch after all.

Macabre authors Stephen King and Clive Barker have continued to be an industry unto themselves, as attested to by a string of best-selling novels and the popular films *Sleepwalkers* and *Misery* (King) and *Hellraiser III* and *Candyman* (Barker). Their thoughts on the nature of fear, their careers and creativity are illuminating and inspiring.

On the FX side of things, nothing can hold back the imagination of Horrorwood's makeup and visual FX wizards anymore, thanks to new, widely-publicized technological breakthroughs. *Gremlins 2: The New Batch*, *Total Recall* and *Terminator 2: Judgment Day* are just three films in which the fantasies of the filmmakers became plausible realities for audiences through the magic of celluloid.

Horror movies have been a form of entertainment since the beginning of the motion picture industry. With the explosion of video and cable outlets today, more people than ever before are enjoying the fears in the night. Now that's something to scream about!

Anthony Timpone

© Columbia

© New Line

© Orion

COPPOLA'S NEW TAKE ON THE CLASSIC NOVEL ADDS A STUNNING ORIGIN PROLOGUE.

THE MASTER OF "BRAM STOKER'S DRACULA"

BY BILL WARREN

All Dracula photos © Columbia

DRACULA FINDS HIS LATEST MEAL TO BE RAZOR-LICKIN' GOOD.

Make no mistake about it: The fact that Francis Ford Coppola, one of the world's greatest film artists, directed *Bram Stoker's Dracula* has no parallel in cinematic history. "Here I am," says Coppola, "doing this 100-year-old novel that's been made 50 billion times, to the point where people think it's camp. Obviously, the first question I've had to answer is, 'Why are you doing it?' And I have to say, 'I thought I could take the novel, which had never quite been done, and get a group of creative people together and come up with something that would, hopefully, live on its own terms."

And make no mistake about his position in the hierarchy of film greats: Coppola's career has careened from the triumphs of the *Godfather* movies, *The Conversation* and *Apocalypse Now* to work-for-hire projects like *Peggy Sue Got Married* and *Gardens of Stone* to projects-gone-awry such as *One From the Heart* and *The Cotton Club*. There is no one like him in film history: a genius of a director who also produces movies, and the courageous head of his own studio (American Zoetrope) who does films for other companies—like Columbia Pictures, for whom he made *Dracula*.

He was first introduced to James V. Hart's script by actress Winona Ryder, who plays Mina in the film. She was originally cast as Michael Corleone's daughter in *Godfather III*, but fell ill and couldn't appear in the movie. "When I thought about it months later," Coppola explains, "I didn't want there to be a situation with an obviously talented young person who had felt bad about dropping out at literally the last moment. So I thought it would be a good idea to meet her a year later, to not let her feel that I hated her or anything. In the course of that meeting, we talked about a number of things. I was talking to her about *On the Road*, but she had brought along a script she wanted me to read."

When he was 18, Coppola had been a drama counselor at a summer camp, where he read Stoker's *Dracula* to the boys in his charge, sending them to shuddering sleep. Much later, Hart's script immediately caught his attention. "It was pretty authentic," Coppola says of the screenplay. "I had fantasized years before about doing *Frankenstein* based on the Mary Shelley novel, with the feeling that the book hadn't quite been done—although *Bride of Frankenstein* is a great movie. So I had had a bee in my bonnet about doing one of the classic Gothic romances, or horror pieces."

With the appearance of Hart's already-written script, Coppola found himself with the opportunity to realize his dark dream. That it had been brought to him by Ryder also put a few ideas into his head. "I thought of doing it with a really young cast," Coppola says. "There was already a script. With *Frankenstein*, I was going to do the script myself, so that was seven months saved right there." While on a trip to Japan, Coppola got a call saying that Columbia wanted to do *Dracula*; though he'd only expressed some interest in the project, Coppola decided to go ahead. "I figured, well, this could be fun, especially if it didn't cost too much money."

Given Coppola's participation in the project, it was inevitable that the film would develop beyond Hart's original script. After all, he is considered by some to be the most daring of American filmmakers. His longtime friend George Lucas (whose first film, *THX-1138*, was produced by Coppola) once said that when they reach the cliffs of life, Lucas lowers a rope ladder and climbs down, while Coppola jumps off.

With *Bram Stoker's Dracula*, the director is making one of his most daring leaps. It's not the movie the world might have expected: Not only does it follow the book far more closely than any other movie ever has, but it boasts a startlingly original visual design and an imaginative, challenging approach to the story. Coppola feels that audiences should not be shortchanged by just another retread of the same old thing, but are worthy of something beautiful, new and dangerous.

KEANU REEVES, FORMERLY HALF OF BILL & TED, FINDS HIMSELF IN THE CLUTCHES OF MORE BABES THAN HE CAN HANDLE.

"A lot of the way I am and what I do is different from other people," Coppola admits. "I'm not such a linear person; I kind of see a project all in one vague impression, and I have a hard time relating that to others. That's why I like to work with collaborators who know me. I get a take on it, almost a spatial intuition of what it might be like—I see it all at once, but not clearly enough so it's easy for me to explain it to the people who have to build it."

Coppola and Hart worked together and with others over a period of time to shape the script into what Coppola had envisioned. The director did thorough research on his material, later testing the script in a staged reading held at a San Francisco restaurant/theater. "We had some actors read the script to people to try it out and hear how it all went down for a contemporary audience," he recalls. "I'm looking for ways to get a connection with the audience, obviously. I was a theater director, and we always used to have those two weeks of previews or rehearsals where you could really see the work going down in front of the audience. I always got a lot of great ideas, and felt, almost for the first time, that I understood what I was doing, shaping it while I could still change it. So always with film, I've struggled to find ways to make it more like the creation of theater."

Coppola also used improvisation and theater games to allow his talented cast to get to know their characters beyond the bounds of ordinary readings and rehearsals—another way in which the project evolved. "But really," Coppola says, "if you read the very first script, and read the text as it is in the film, you could say that on the one hand it changed, but on the other it didn't. The original script was full of dialogue and scenes; we tried to slim it down, but as it is, the movie has over 60 scenes and sets."

Aside from the compression of incident which occurs every time a novel is adapted for the screen, the two major differences between the plot of Stoker's novel and the finished film can be found in the character of Professor Abraham Van Helsing (Anthony Hopkins) and in the strong romance between Dracula and Mina.

"Van Helsing is such a fuddy-duddy in the novel, this kindly, innocent old guy, and he isn't a very interesting character," Coppola elaborates. "We came up with the idea of Van Helsing as a kind of Goethe, a guy who drank, and went to bawdy houses, and got into duels—much more salty, kind of like Walter Huston in *Treasure of the Sierra Madre*. We evolved that out of Tony's improvisation, which influenced the character a lot."

While researching the novel and the historical Vlad the Impaler, Hart discovered that when one of Dracula's wives was falsely told he'd died in the battle with the Turks, she drowned herself (the Transylvanian river in which this occurred is still named for the event). Taking a page from history and incorporating it into Stoker's mythos, Hart created a twist which does not appear in the novel: In his script, Mina turns out to be the reincarnation of this wife, Dracula's long-lost love. Her death is, in fact, what leads Dracula to challenge God and results in his becoming a vampire. In this way, his encounter with Mina in turn-of-the-century London is both a centerpiece in Coppola's film and the story's driving force. Though it is indeed a major change, Coppola feels that the variation stays true to the novel's spirit. "Jim Hart's innovation was that love story based on history," Coppola says. "We call it *Bram Stoker's Dracula*, and it's very truthful to Stoker.

"I thought that was a positive innovation," Coppola adds, "in that it gives you a handle to treat the whole story in a way that had never been done before—and yet allows you to do the Stoker piece. You could sink your teeth into it a little better," he says, using some of his own vampiric imagery. "It was Stoker's great innovation to endow a historical figure such as Vlad with this vampire phenomenon. So Jim took that

one step further, and brought in even more of the historical Dracula.''

Those additions necessitated a change in the main character's motivation. "The main business of Dracula in this version is the passion that drove this love affair," the director says. "Even though he could be sympathetic in that you understand his passion, it's almost that by renouncing God, he becomes all the more evil—because like the fallen angel Lucifer, he was once good."

Dracula, therefore, must remain both evil and attractive for the story to work. This is always true in productions of *Dracula*, and Coppola hoped to extend these ideas with the increased emphasis on the timeless romance. "We all know those kind of love stories," Coppola says, "like *Romeo and Juliet, Tristan and Isolde*, these incredibly tragic love affairs. The script came up with a pair of lovers along that line, so we wanted it to have that passion.

"It's true that those elements don't normally go with a Gothic horror film," the director admits, "and I did go right on the nose with horror—you really see these monsters, and they're spewing bile and stuff, so it's not as though it's a psychological interpretation of the novel. Gothic horror has always had love and romance in it, as in the Edgar Allan Poe films, but not with the two coexisting as much as they do in this film. Obviously, part of our calculation is that those two elements can be compatible, the love story occasionally punctuated by moments of horror."

But ultimately, Dracula is evil, and so he must die at the film's climax. "At his moment of death, he does die as a mortal, which is something I liked. I didn't want him to die in a dissolving blob of spit, blood and rage, so I had him die very simply, very Christlike. But in the making of it, I didn't do it quite exactly like the script, so there is a little something extra that happens."

**TOP LEFT
AS HE ENTERS
CASTLE DRACULA,
THE VAMPIRE
BRIDES GIVE HARKER
A TASTE OF FANGS
TO COME.**

**TOP RIGHT
THE EXTENSIVE
MAKEUP BY GREG
CANNOM AND CREW
PROVIDES THE
BELOVED
BLOODSUCKER A
'90S SENSIBILITY.**

Coppola is one of the great casting directors of all time; looking at the credits of *The Godfather* and *The Outsiders*, one will recall that the majority of the actors in both films were relatively unknown when the movies were made—Al Pacino and Tom Cruise being but two examples. So it's not surprising that the *Dracula* roster includes not only Ryder and Hopkins, but Keanu Reeves, Cary Elwes, Richard E. Grant and Bill Campbell as well. Coppola's most surprising stroke, however, was the casting of Dracula himself: Gary Oldman, known in the U.S. primarily for playing Lee Harvey Oswald in *JFK*.

"It's a problem when there isn't someone available who immediately fits all the bills," Coppola explains. "Like if there was a guy as handsome as Errol Flynn and as good at doing grotesquerie as Lon Chaney—but in the end, there *wasn't* an actor who fit all the requirements. I just kind of went with who would put the most unique stamp on it, and give it the most individual touch. If you're going to do *Dracula*, you want to at least have people say, 'The guy who plays Dracula is terrific! I never saw anything like that.' And I feel you'll say that when you see Gary."

The rest of the cast began filming before it was necessary for Oldman to begin shooting his scenes, and so the actor was left without much to do. "He was hanging around, dying to work, but he was spending time with the makeup and costume people and constantly coming up with ideas," Coppola recalls. "I'd get a call from him: 'I got this great idea! And the producer said we might be able to use it! So can we go ahead?' Gary's a creative guy; he kept getting sequestered with [makeup FX creator] Greg Cannom and coming up with new makeup ideas."

Even the withered, ancient but still powerful Dracula we meet in the opening scenes is something new to films. Christopher Lee tried a similar approach in Jess Franco's unfortunate *Count Dracula*, but don't expect that image in this version. "We imagined him as being very old," Coppola explains, "existing in a culture between the East and West, right there next to the Ottoman Empire; Dracula was definitely an eastern Byzantine prince." In fact, the historical Vlad Dracula had been held hostage by the Turks, and had grown up among them. "I encouraged Eiko Ishioka, the costume designer, to use the Byzantine elements. At first, Dracula had a Fu Manchu kind of straggling beard. We looked at him with and without this, and I kind of dug the androgynous look. He could almost be an old woman; it seemed to be haunting, and I went for it."

Coppola had first envisioned a very experimental approach to *Dracula*. But when the film was shot on the studio lot in Culver City, the director was faced with a major difficulty: He was not working with his usual partners, such as production designer Dean Tavoularis and cinematographer Vittorio Storaro. He was tremendously pleased, however, with the work the great German director of photography Michael Ballhaus did on *Dracula*. "Ballhaus did a *wonderful* job," Coppola emphasizes.

"When you're working on a movie, it's like you're the general of an army," Coppola continues. "When you don't know the officers and noncomissioned officers and soldiers so well, and they're already enlisted, they have a way of doing things. The prop people do props the way it's done for a big studio, and the stuntpeople do stunts that way." This is why studio movies look so much alike; Coppola cites Jean-Luc Godard's comment that if the credits were cut off most movies, no one could tell who made them.

The studio system was particularly troublesome concerning the film's sets. "They kept getting bigger," Coppola says, "and I kept slapping them down—even to the point of firing one art director, because they wouldn't believe me when I said I wanted to do certain scenes in shadow, or with volumes of empty soundstages without a lot of sets, using opaque projections. The set budget on its own kept getting bigger and bigger; I never wanted a big look for the settings, I wanted more of an imaginative suggestion, but basically I got a big look. I wasn't capable of stopping that."

Coppola's new approach to *Dracula* might have intimidated the studio a little. "Although ideas are titillating," he says, "as it gets closer to the day when you're gonna do it, they tend to resort more to what they know. Partly, it may be that they don't really believe you're going to go that far out." And far out is where the director has gone. Many of the special FX, which were under the direction of Alison Savitch and Coppola's son Roman, were done live on the set, or in old-fashioned ways, partly to match the period of the film. This vintage feel extends to the visuals, which were influenced not by current Hollywood films, but by past masters of the medium. "It was influenced by Jean [*Beauty and the Beast*] Cocteau, by F.W. [*Nosferatu*] Murnau, by Pabst, quite a few of the filmmakers of the early '20s [though Cocteau was later], partly because their approach to effects was live-action, magic illusion tricks.

"My approach was sort of surrealist in that it was based on symbolist paintings— the kind with a girl, which also contain the obelisk, the eye, the clock, the symbols that are precursors of surrealism. And of course Cocteau was a surrealist, so all that way of looking at it definitely influenced me.

"The irony," Coppola concludes, "is that even though this film didn't turn out as experimental as I originally planned—I got maybe 40 percent of what I was going for —it's still not your conventional movie. Certain aspects of it got away from me, got bigger than I intended; I was looking at making a smaller, stranger, artier version, and what I got is a *big*, strange, artier version. It's one of a kind—but I guess that's good. It's Francis Coppola's version of *Dracula*, the drama counselor who finally got to direct the book."

DIRECTOR COPPOLA PROMISES TO LET TOM WAITS OUT OF HIS CELL IF HE STOPS MAKING FUN OF WINONA RYDER'S PERIOD OUTFIT.

WHY "SILENCE" WAS GOLDEN

BY ANTHONY C. FERRANTE

While horror films are slowly running out of inventive new ways to dismember, decapitate and emasculate screen victims, the genre is turning to more intellectual methods of frightening moviegoers. Director Jonathan Demme's suspense thriller *The Silence of the Lambs* (based on the best-selling novel by Thomas Harris) takes this approach, leading the audience into the horribly twisted world of incarcerated sociopath Hannibal "The Cannibal" Lecter.

Silence of the Lambs is a rare thriller in that it exploits the psychological as opposed to the physical side of horror in ways the screen has infrequently touched upon in the past. That's due in part to the deliriously wicked tapestry spun in the Harris novel, faithfully transposed to the screen by playwright Ted Tally and given life by Demme's inspired direction.

"I believe we nailed the book," says Demme. "This stuff is so gripping that even if they know what happens, people will just come unglued anyway."

Demme is yet another New World Pictures alumnus from the '70s, and quickly learned the Roger Corman rules of low-budget etiquette on his directorial debut, the tongue-in-cheek women-behind-bars schlocker *Caged Heat*. Yet unlike many Corman grads who went on to have significant impact on the horror genre, Demme went in the opposite direction and made the touching dramas *Melvin and Howard* and *Handle With Care*, as well as the manic comedies *Something Wild* and *Married to the Mob*. *Silence of the Lambs* marks the first time Demme has ventured into the dark side of the cinema, and he proves capable of serving up a healthy dose of disturbing onscreen viscera, ranging from skinned corpses to the strikingly bloody messes Dr. Lecter leaves behind after his fiendishly clever prison escape.

All *Silence of the Lamb* photos © Orion

A neophyte in the horror arena, Demme was concerned about going overboard with the film's violence. He attempted to balance the grisly elements so that they didn't overpower the film's intense, psychological rhythm. "Any filmmaker has an ongoing relationship with screen violence, and if you care about violence in society as I do, you inevitably wind up in some kind of conflict with yourself about it," Demme muses. "My basic struggle is wanting to be very responsible and show violence, when it's called for, as something horrifying and demeaning. Even though I know better, the little kid moviegoer in me who grew up loving Westerns and war movies still sticks his head out and gets carried away with thrilling action scenes. I never get thrilled anymore if there's some kind of orgiastic, pornographic, bullet-spraying violence like *Rambo*—violence for violence's sake. But if it's in a movie that's professing to have a theme of integrity, and it's one of those big showdown kind of moments, I can get swept up by that.

"I failed at that a lot in *Married to the Mob* by trying to do some exciting, thrilling gunfights. I think I'm a lot more successful in my struggle with this movie. This picture, as far as I'm concerned, is anti-violence. It's not a movie that invites you to cheer at violence; it's a movie that makes you dread it."

Not only did *Lambs* liberate Demme from the restraints of comedy, it also gave him ample opportunity to develop a rich, dramatic environment for these strong characters to squirm in. "It was beautiful to just say, 'Is this scene real?' and not 'Is this scene real and is it funny?' " Demme enthuses. "These aren't funny times now, and who's in the mood for laughing? It's important to see movies that help us get even more upset than we are from reading the newspapers."

At the core of *Silence of the Lambs* is not so much unrelenting violence, but the mental warfare engaged by Dr. Lecter (Anthony Hopkins) and FBI trainee Clarice Starling (Jodie Foster). Starling is on the trail of a serial killer nicknamed Buffalo Bill (because he skins his victims) and needs Lecter's expertise on the criminal mind to track him down. Demme feels that what makes Lecter so effectively bone-chilling is the fact

**TOP LEFT
IN *Silence of the
Lambs*, JODIE FOSTER
CREATES THE KIND
OF STRONG,
SYMPATHETIC
HEROINE THE
MOVIES HAVE LONG
NEEDED.**

**TOP RIGHT
THE CHILLING
PSYCHIC WARFARE
BETWEEN CLARICE
AND LECTER
RESULTED IN THE
YEAR'S MOST
MEMORABLE SCREEN
SHIVERS.**

that he is quite human, and that Hopkins somehow brings out the disarming charms of the character while hinting at the quiet madness inside.

"I felt Tony would be fantastic for Dr. Lecter for two basic reasons," Demme comments. "One, he's a person who projects extreme intelligence. There's something about him that makes you feel, in my case anyway, that this man is a lot smarter than you are—and of course that is fundamental to Lecter. I also felt that the other quality Tony has is a great humanity and passion, especially in *The Elephant Man*."

Hopkins is no stranger to psychologically unbalanced characters either. He played the tragically disturbed ventriloquist in 1978's *Magic* as well as the harried father in the 1977 supernatural thriller *Audrey Rose*. Lecter, however, is Hopkins' crowning achievement, becoming one of the screen's most charismatic and dynamic antiheroes since Norman Bates refused to harm a fly.

"I've spoken to Hopkins a few times recently, and he's still Dr. Lecter," smiles Demme. "Tony just got the joke of Dr. Lecter in a way nobody, save perhaps Tom Harris, may have gotten him."

In preparing for this arduous role, Hopkins avoided the Method approach, since he admits to having taken that style of acting a little too seriously early on in his career. He feels that audiences don't care how involved an actor gets with his role, explaining that you could spend "four months in a mental ward, but all the audience cares about is the performance.

"The thing about playing a part like Hannibal Lecter or Adolf Hitler is that you must always look for the opposite side of them—you look for the sympathetic side if possible," Hopkins offers. "Lecter is sophisticated, erudite and a smooth charmer—a seducer. So you play that side of him and let the audience decide.

"Lecter is so in control of everything," Hopkins continues. "He can hear every sound in that prison block. He can smell Clarice Starling as she's coming down the corridor. He's not the devil. He can't anticipate the moves of everyone else. He's just so honest—and that's the horror of the man. Anyone who can be that perceptive has to be mad."

Though Hopkins didn't spend time doing tedious research on sociopaths, he did use several visualizations to create the cool mannerisms that give Lecter his memorable screen presence. He says that first came the "ambivalent voice," which he describes as a cross between Katharine Hepburn and Truman Capote. Next came a visual understanding of what the name Hannibal Lecter stood for.

"The thing that really got me was the name Lecter," Hopkins details. "The image I got was this ebony desk and inside were killing instruments—knives. And that, in fact, Lecter was a killing machine—he was his own name. And with Hannibal I thought of a praying mantis—somebody who is so sturdy that you wonder if he's awake. So what I did was stand very still and use my eyes a lot."

Another chilling aspect of Lecter's ominous nature is his clothing. He may be locked inside a cell that resembles a Gothic dungeon, but Lecter's all-white wardrobe adds a stark contrast to his surroundings. Hopkins says that costume designer Colleen Atwood was initially going to have him dressed in orange, but convinced her that a white shirt, white pants and white shoes would add a clinical malevolence to Lecter. Hopkins' inspiration was a childhood fear of dentists.

"I remember the first time I'd ever been to a dentist, and there was a man all in white and he was so frightening," Hopkins laughs. "So I saw Lecter in white, to make him really terrifying."

Lecter may be the centerpiece of *Lambs'* intricate web of darkness, but Demme found himself more "infatuated" with the character of Clarice Starling. Demme has high praise for Jodie Foster for bringing Clarice to life, and adds that this is the first part the Academy Award-winning actress has performed where she hasn't had to "mask her intelligence."

Foster was drawn to the role primarily because Starling is a heroine who shows some depth and vulnerability—something she feels is virtually extinct from films today. "This is the first time we've really seen a female hero who isn't running around in her underwear going 'aggg' or isn't some kind of steroid version of a man," Foster says.

The actress didn't rehearse her mesmerizing verbal interchanges with Hopkins, and she found that although those scenes were fun to shoot, she was completely drained afterwards. She believes that the key to making those scenes work was the respect that Clarice and Lecter have for each other, though they may not subscribe to each other's philosophies. "Dignity is the thread between the two of them—Lecter is looking for human dignity and so is she," Foster maintains. "Clarice has the respect for him that allows her to see him as a human being. She's not judgmental. That doesn't mean she condones his behavior, or that she doesn't fear him or feel that he should be locked up forever."

Silence of the Lambs isn't the first time Thomas Harris' Lecter character has made a gripping impression on the screen. In 1986, Harris' novel *Red Dragon* was transformed into *Manhunter*, with Brian Cox (a friend of Hopkins, no less) bringing Lecter to life. Though Harris has provided a memorable and distinguished villain for horror fans, Demme says that the popular novelist is very nervous about seeing his beloved characters living on screen, apprehensive that an actor might rob his creation of his charms and prevent the author from writing about him again.

It's doubtful that this will happen anytime soon, and Demme hints that Harris may have another Dr. Lecter story in the works. "I'm sure it's not anything as neat as a sequel," Demme adds. "I'm already lobbying to direct the next Harris novel, with or without these characters—but especially with them."

BERNARD ROSE'S DEMONS OF THE MIND

BY DANIEL SCHWEIGER

rson Welles once remarked that film was a "ribbon of dreams," the audiences' escapist beliefs powering their celluloid fantasies. But director Bernard Rose's cinema is an unrelenting nightmare, and sleep is the quicksand that pulls his characters towards their ultimate confrontation with evil.

From a little girl drawing *Paperhouse*'s twisted dreamscape to the movie-entrenched murder spree of *Chicago Joe and the Showgirl*, Rose's ominous visions don't so much entice viewers as hypnotize them. His surreal and calculating techniques make audiences doubt the safety of their movie theater, the director's mind games ripping apart the barrier between escapist fantasies and real terror. But first, Rose's victims must subconsciously wish for their darkest imaginings to come true.

When the beautiful researcher Helen jokingly calls out the name of an urban bogeyman, she invites a lovestruck creature who won't return to his dreamworld until Helen agrees to be his victim.

Candyman is the British director's third and most haunting film, adapting Clive Barker's short story "The Forbidden" into a malefic love story. The author had created a walking nightmare, a hook-handed,

Paperhouse **WAS DIRECTOR ROSE'S FIRST CINEMATIC BAD DREAM.**

bee-filled phantom who splits his prey from "nob to gullet." Yet "The Forbidden" drew on Barker's literate side, not his blood-splattered one, revealing society's undying fascination for ghoulish fables.

Mesmerized by the power of its myths, Rose immediately bought the rights from Barker. With the author aboard as executive producer, Rose's newly-titled *Candyman* changed the setting from a Liverpool slum to Chicago's Cabrini Green, a blighted housing project that would give the killer a horrifyingly real lair. Rose's screenplay also gave the story feature-length flesh by exploring the past lives of Helen and Candyman. Once a cultured black artist and his smitten white model, their forbidden affair in the 1800s led to his horrible murder. When Candyman returns to claim a reincarnated Helen's affections, her refusal causes the enraged soulmate to frame her for murder.

Though his fatal attraction doesn't skimp on Barker's S&M fetishes, Rose's take

on the writer is unexpectedly subtle. "Most people don't realize that Clive's a novelist, and not just a slasher writer," the director says. "While Stephen King writes pulp fiction with one eye on what sells, Barker sees his stories as literature."

Rose's disdain for most modern horror films helped him to avoid clichés in scripting *Candyman*. "There's a postmodernist thing where every movie has eaten itself," Rose says. "People sit around regurgitating ideas, and their ideas are second-hand. I'm glad not to have seen any of the *Nightmare on Elm Street* films, since the only way to avoid clichés is by not making a film that's based on other movies. And it's important to have a concrete vision of the film before you start, because you've got to be directing for the actors once you're on stage. That way, they'll give you far more than was ever conceived on paper."

Though Rose's *Candyman* plays on ghetto horrors to a far greater extent than does Barker's story, the director sees his film as a dissection of "urban legends" instead of a supernatural class struggle. "*Candyman*'s thrust is metaphysical instead of political," he says. "My element of social criticism asks how people can be expected to live in squalor, because the housing authority has allowed Cabrini Green to rot instead of trying to maintain it. But *Candyman* really poses the question that if God exists because we believe in him, what would happen to him if the worship ceased? Would there be a five-minute period where God is running on belief, and would he try to win his followers back? People have a deep need to believe in something beyond themselves, especially when they're living in an appalling place like Cabrini Green. They could be shot at any time, but a creature like Candyman could do something far worse to them. That belief allows the people to dodge bullets in the stairwells."

Though the residents pay Candyman tribute with razor-laced sweets, Helen tries to convince his "congregation" that their hushed rumors of castrations and disembowelments are just childrens' tales. When she "reveals" Candyman to be a gang member's hoax, the true spirit appears to show Helen how real he is. And in Rose's Hitchcockian setup, only Helen can see the ghost that's murdering anyone who might believe her. "I wanted *Candyman* to say that the supernatural exists, but it's done entirely from Helen's perspective as she goes 'crazy,' " the director explains. "Yet I didn't want to make Candyman into a monster. He's a melancholic, mysterious figure who has to kill people. When he writes 'It was always you, Helen' in his lair, it's a double-edged statement. He could be referring to their lives in the 1890s, or making Helen think she was slaying people as Candyman."

Once Rose had cast Tony Todd and Virginia Madsen as Candyman and Helen, the filmmaker encouraged them to create their characters' pasts, a blood history which

**CANDYMAN GOES UP
IN FLAMES, BUT NOT
WITHOUT A FIGHT.**

he incorporated into the film. But Rose's most chilling preparation was to hypnotize Madsen for her scenes with the villain. "*Candyman*'s pivotal moment is when he first appears to Helen," he says. "Up until then, the movie has been a detective story. But once we know Candyman exists, the rules instantly change. I wanted to avoid the horror cliché of having the heroine scream and run away. How many thousands of times have we seen that done badly? Since I felt Candyman would hypnotize his prey, I wanted Helen to be on another level of experience when confronting him. During rehearsals, I'd get Virginia into a trance by having her relax and talking to her. Then once we were on the set, I could use key phrases to trigger her hypnosis."

A fan of *The Exorcist* and *Rosemary's Baby*, Rose expanded on the subliminal tricks of William Friedkin and Roman Polanski. Using glimpses of Candyman's lair and his "unhooked" victims, the film's rapid editing lures audiences into Helen's trance, convincing them that the phantom is everywhere when in fact his screen time is relatively brief. Rose insisted upon using "natural film magic" instead of state-of-the-art visuals to accomplish these tricks.

"Your eyes don't work like a movie camera, because things are much more sudden and impressionistic than how you interpret them," he says. "But the more you familiarize viewers with the supernatural, the harder it is to maintain your threat. The shark in *Jaws* looked like rubber the more you saw it, while *Terminator 2*'s morphing is now in every crappy film. That made it important to shoot Candyman as realistically as possible, without smoke or computer-generated opticals."

Rose helped to devise several impressive on-set FX during *Candyman*'s shoot in Chicago and LA. While bee wrangler Norman Gary stuffed insects into Todd's mouth, FX coordinator Martin Bresin built a levitation rig for Candyman to float over a strapped-down Helen, wires hurling Todd out of the hospital window when she screams. In addition to shooting gushers of blood, makeup artist Bob Keen constructed three hooks for Todd's meaty stump. The film's climax required three bonfires, as Helen and Candyman have their showdown in a flaming pile of trash, metal supports imploding the rubble on cue.

ROSE'S DOOMED HEROINE MAKES THE ULTIMATE SACRIFICE IN *Candyman's* FIERY CONCLUSION.

All *Candyman* photos © TriStar

Sadly, however, Rose's most dexterous camera feat wouldn't survive his merciless editing. In one of Candyman's few moments of tenderness, the phantom literally sweeps Helen off her feet, waltzing his old flame across the ghetto lair. "I based my script around that image," Rose sighs. "But the waltz seemed superfluous and over-stated once I edited the film. It was like telling the audience, 'In case you didn't get it, Candyman's in love with Helen.' "

Sound would be one of the last ingredients in Rose's terrifying scheme, utilizing the hum of a thousand bees and the decaying crashes of Cabrini Green. George Lucas' facilities were also used to create Candyman's sonorous voice, a hellish echo that wraps around the screen whenever he appears. Yet it was the eerie music of Philip (Koyaanisqatsi) Glass that finally shaped the movie, his tubular voices helping to turn Candyman into an unholy church mass. While other directors might show their com-poser the final cut and pray for the best, Rose brought in Glass to see his first rushes.

"The music became an integral part of Candyman instead of an afterthought," Rose says. "Unlike a traditional 'horror' score, I wanted Philip to create the tension instead of the 'stings.' Music should unsettle viewers without pulverizing them, and audiences have become used to droning synthesizers that tell them when a monster's going to jump out. Because Candyman's soundtrack doesn't alert you to the threat, every scene has the potential for something unpleasant to happen."

Before getting his feature film break with 1988's Paperhouse, Rose's background was in the blasting percussion of rock videos, doing shorts for such acts as Frankie Goes to Hollywood, UB40 and Roy Orbison. As he applied his MTV-learned low-budget resourcefulness to provide Paperhouse with its slick appearance, Rose found his terror's wellspring in dreams. As a pubescent girl retreats into her personal twilight zone, the director locked onto his theme of imagination spiraling out of control as she begins playing God with her crippled, imaginary boyfriend and a demonic father-figure. The real world is a pawn of the character's nightmares, its individuals failing to realize that they've been caught in a dark dream until it's too late.

"I like the idea of a story where the character appears to do nothing," Rose smiles. "Paperhouse has a little girl getting sick for a few weeks. Then she gets better and goes to the seaside. Yet no one realizes that she's going through a huge conflict with her 'father.' Childhood is often romanticized as a wonderful thing, but most people really hated being kids. They weren't taken seriously, and the girl in Paperhouse regards the adults around her as jailers. There are no possibilities for her unless she grows up. So in a sense, she has to kill the father to make love. Paperhouse is basically about sex, with big phallic objects that stick out of the ground. Then the kids finally get to the biggest one of all, which is the lighthouse."

With some of the most imaginative dream imagery since Jean Cocteau's Beauty and the Beast, Paperhouse won the grand prize at France's Avoriaz Film Festival. But the critical acclaim did little to bring in an audience, as the movie's high-concept distributor was confounded by Rose's unique vision. "While Paperhouse got me an agent in Hollywood, it was a tough picture for Vestron to sell," he says. "People didn't know if it was a horror film or a kids' movie, and I certainly didn't have any idea how to market it. I always viewed Paperhouse as a psychological story, and was very sur-prised when people told me how frightening it was. So maybe it should have been sold to the horror audience. But there are always three reactions to a film: the critical one, the money it takes in and how it's regarded years later. It's the third one that's most important to me, and more people like Paperhouse now than when it came out."

It became even more difficult to label Rose after Chicago Joe and the Showgirl, a wildly uneven thriller about a gangster-obsessed American GI (Kiefer Sutherland) and his affair with a starry-eyed Cockney dancer (Emily Lloyd) during World War II. Unable to consummate their attraction, their passion instead erupts into a series of bloody crimes across England. Though true to the lurid facts, *Chicago Joe* was as much of a dark fantasy as *Paperhouse*, the showgirl envisioning the robberies as if she were a film noir lover on the lam. "I really don't know what to think of it," Rose confides. "After the screening, I thought, 'My God, this film is berserk!' It purports to be a docudrama about a 1940s murder, but the film's really a Hollywood musical."

Rose staged the movie's violence with deliberately overwrought humor, an operatic chorus blasting over buzz-bomb victims while a grisly murder attempt takes place in front of an obvious studio backdrop. Yet the killings are full of agony, a visceral approach that Rose also applies to *Candyman*'s discreetly shocking murders.

"There's a pact kept with the audience in a Schwarzenegger movie, because they're witnessing destruction without pain. But I've always liked to be nasty with my audience, and make them feel *pain* in a murder. When a woman's head gets smashed in *Chicago Joe*, she's still standing up, not realizing what's happened. But as soon as the viewers know something's gone wrong, they get terrified."

Rose has made sure *Candyman* is a thrill ride with no escape. Like *Alien³*, the film creates an escalating sense of doom by putting its heroine through torture. Rose's fatalistic horror is a deliberate refusal to give the audience another optimistic cliché, and helped determine his choice of film genres.

"Tragedy is one of the great dramatic forms, but Hollywood has a terrible straitjacket on now," Rose says. "They'll bowdlerize *Cyrano de Bergerac* as *Roxanne*, but what's the point if he gets the girl instead of dying? Could you imagine a studio doing *King Lear*? The finale would have him weeping over Cordelia. Then she'd come back to life, embrace Lear, build him an old-age home and then run the kingdom! Everything has got to climax with people hugging each other, and saying, 'I love you, Mom,' and 'I love you, Dad.' Films have become an orgy of butt-kissing, and if you try to do something different, your film will be reshot. So I worked out that the only way to make a tragedy in Hollywood was to call it horror.

"There's a certain stigma attached to thrillers, and that's what attracted me to them," Rose continues. "Some people in town regard it as half a notch above hardcore porn. But morality doesn't matter in those pictures, since you can screw everyone and not get killed for it! I've always liked that, and the glorious thing about horror is that you don't have to hug everyone. In fact, this is the only genre where you can kill the entire cast!"

Rose hopes that Hollywood will label him as one of its "mad" visionaries, a director who's lauded for his eccentricity. "I'm a big fan of David Cronenberg, because he uses the excuse of horror to do things that he couldn't get away with in a straight drama. You have to carve a niche like he did. But for better or worse, I've never made a film that wasn't mine. I'm not interested in doing films that are determined by market research. They're too hard and boring. A movie is only interesting if you see that the director has a point of view, and makes you see the world in a different way. Our perception of what's 'real' is very subjective, and the way I see life is slightly out of step from traditional filmmaking."

MISERY'S COMPANY

BY ANTHONY C. FERRANTE

THE THREE FACES OF ANNIE, AS SCULPTED BY THE KNB EFX TEAM.

Misery is in the eye of the beholder.

Just ask Annie Wilkes (Kathy Bates), who's nursing her favorite romance novelist, Paul Sheldon (James Caan), back to health after a near-fatal road accident. Luckily for him, she's his "number-one fan." Unluckily for him, she's not very stable and gets mighty disturbed when she discovers he's killed off her favorite character, Misery Chastain, in his latest book. She gets so upset, in fact, that she's willing to do anything to force Sheldon to resurrect Misery from pulp death—even murder.

So goes the premise of one of 1990's most successful horror films, *Misery*, which grossed more than $61 million at the box office, garnered Kathy Bates an Academy Award for Best Actress, provided one of the finest adaptations of a Stephen King novel to date and proved that even former sitcom-stars-turned-directors like Rob Reiner know a thing or two about scaring audiences.

"The main thing that was difficult for me was the film's genre," reveals Reiner, whose other films include *This is Spinal Tap*, *The Princess Bride* and *When Harry Met Sally*. . . . "I had never done anything of this type, and at times I questioned whether I could pull it off. And as it turns out, the fact that I hadn't done anything like this and basically came to it in a different way made it a nice kind of weird marriage of comedy and suspense-thriller. The biggest question for us was: Are Stephen King fans going to like the movie, even though it isn't really a typical Stephen King film?"

Obtaining the movie rights to the book turned out to be an easier task than anticipated. King had been skeptical about selling it to a studio for some time, fearing that it would be butchered like many of his other works. Also, *Misery* was a book very

All *Misery* photos © Columbia

DIRECTOR REINER
ORCHESTRATES A
SCENE IN *Misery's*
CLAUSTROPHOBIC
BEDROOM SET.

close to his heart, so he was overprotective of it. But he trusted Reiner, who directed the 1986 sleeper hit *Stand By Me*, an excellent adaptation of the novella "The Body" from his *Different Seasons* collection. The only catch was that, before King would sign over the rights, Reiner would have to attach his name as either producer or director.

"I wouldn't know how to begin to direct *Pet Sematary* or *Cujo*—I'm not interested in them," Reiner says. "The elements that draw me to his pieces have nothing to do with what most people are drawn to. I don't like horror movies and I don't like supernatural things, and most of his books deal with horror and the supernatural. I can't connect with that. *Stand By Me* was very atypical: There was no horror. I liked the character of Gordy. And with *Misery* I was drawn to Paul Sheldon. So that's what interested me, not so much, 'Ooooh, let's do a horror movie.' "

Ultimately, Reiner decided to direct the film himself and started rounding up his core film family. Barry Sonnenfeld returned as cinematographer (after doing *When Harry Met Sally . . .*) and William Goldman was asked to adapt King's book following his successful 1987 collaboration with Reiner on *The Princess Bride*.

"Rob's very script-oriented, and he works extremely hard and very slowly on a screenplay," Goldman explains. "It's an arduous process working with him. It's not like just going to a second or third draft. The thing changes constantly until he's comfortable with it, then he shoots it."

In restructuring the story for the screen, Reiner immediately decided to throw out many of the book's intensely violent scenes, since he felt the movie was about characters, not violence and gore. "This is not a blood-and-guts film," Reiner says firmly. "And that makes it more interesting in a way, because what we've done is very slowly and carefully created real characters, so that when something bad happens to one of them, you feel much more terrified, as opposed to seeing someone offed every five minutes. That's like cartoon violence, when Bugs Bunny gets his head blown off and the next thing you know he's running around and his face is black for a minute, and then it's better again. You become kind of immune to it."

As for Goldman, he was used to bringing novels to the screen, since he's adapted many of his own, ranging from *Marathon Man* to the psychological thriller *Magic*. In addition, he knew that elements of *Misery*'s story had to change in order for it to work successfully on screen, but he also strove to keep the flavor of King's writing intact. Thus, much of Annie's oddball epithets like "oogy" and "dirty bird" were left in. "I was always conscious that it was Steve's baby, and I wanted him to like it," Goldman says. "But it's a 380-page book. It starts off with a character on drugs and in pain trapped by a monster. You get that in the first five pages. My contribution is that it starts very slow, because if we started off high there was no place to go. The book is essentially two people in a room; we were scared about it being claustrophobic."

In order to open up the story a bit, Goldman added the characters of the sheriff and his wife (Richard Farnsworth and Frances Sternhagen), so the film could travel outside the realm of Annie's isolated cabin. A second technique that was considered to broaden the movie's landscape was showing scenes from the Misery Chastain romance novels, but Goldman felt that—even though they were an integral part of the book—they would have detracted from the film's tone.

"About a fifth of the book is a lot of dopey scenes about Misery doing this or Misery getting buried," Goldman recalls. "In the first draft I had three of them, but then we decided we could get away with having the audience understand what the plots of the books were without showing them those scenes. That's tricky and hard to do, but the audience does understand that."

ANNIE MAKES SURE HER CAPTIVE TAKES HIS MEDICINE.

When casting got underway for *Misery*, Warren Beatty was considered for the role of Paul Sheldon. Reiner worked with the actor every day for two months on the script, mainly to refine the character and make him less passive. But in the end, Beatty never signed.

"I got to feel like I'm sure many of his lovers felt—he just couldn't commit," Reiner laughs. "I couldn't get him to the altar, and he wouldn't give me the ring. As it turns out, it was best for everybody, because *Dick Tracy* was coming out at the time and Warren was involved with every bit of advertising and marketing, so he probably would have shown up one day per month to shoot *Misery*."

It was Beatty's involvement, however, that altered one of the book's most chilling scenes: Annie chopping off Sheldon's foot after he tries to escape. In the movie, she breaks his ankles by whacking them with a sledgehammer.

"When Warren first brought this up, I thought it was a star saying, 'I don't want to get my foot cut off,'" Reiner explains. "But it wasn't that. He said, 'I would love to have my foot cut off, but you're writing a story about a character who breaks out of a prison. And do you want to make the statement that in order to grow, you have to lose some-

thing?' And I said, 'I want to make a statement that in order to grow, you have to go through enormous pain, and you come out of that pain even more connected and larger than you were going in.'"

Replacing Beatty was James Caan, who found the role a challenge and at times extremely uncomfortable, since he was required to be bedridden for nearly 90 percent of the movie. "It was like Rob played a sadistic joke and thought, 'Let's get the most hyper person we know and tell him not to move,'" Caan laughs.

As for the part of Annie, Bette Midler had courted the idea of

**PAUL SHELDON
DOESN'T IMAGINE
HE'LL BE SAVED
ANYTIME SOON.**

playing the maladjusted psycho woman, but she was ultimately afraid it might tarnish her image. Reiner, on the other hand, was already convinced that since they were casting a name actor in the role of Sheldon, an unknown should play Annie. In fact, accomplished stage actress Kathy Bates was Goldman's first choice even before he had written a word. He had been fascinated with her stage work in *Frankie and Johnny in the Clair de Lune*, and told Reiner he was going to fashion the role with her in mind.

"I've only written parts for three actors in my life," Goldman states. "I wrote *The Great Waldo Pepper* for Robert Redford, on *The Princess Bride* I rewrote the part of the giant for Andre the Giant, and I wrote this for Kathy Bates. It's an extraordinary performance, and that makes the film terrifying because you don't know who she is. It's not Jessica Lange; it's not Jane Fonda. So Kathy's the secret weapon in this picture. Very rarely in Hollywood does someone her age get a lead in a major motion picture. The thinking out here is that if she's really any good, she would've had her break-through already." Reiner adds, "I'm obviously prejudiced because I made the film, but just looking at it objectively, I can't think of a better performance by a woman this year in an American film." Fittingly, Bates' work on the movie earned her the Best Actress Oscar in 1991.

A fan of "scary movies," Bates thought it was quite appropriate that she got the part, especially since she's read a great deal of King's work over the years and holds *Misery* in the highest regard. *"Misery* was the first novel I read that was really, really special and well-written," she praises. "And when it first came out I had a longing to play the character, because a friend gave me the book and said, "You've got to read this. It's a great character and if they ever make the movie, you should play her.'"

Researching the role of the homely but sharp-tempered Annie, Bates pored over countless books about serial killers, most notably Ted Bundy, Genene Jones (a nurse who murdered children in a hospital) and Diane Downs (a woman who killed her children). Bates also viewed a taped segment from a Geraldo show called "Nurses that Kill," which she felt was important in shaping Annie's character.

"I thought there was only one, but I was surprised that there were a number of people in jail for doing this," Bates says. "There was one guy, and the way he talked was so chilling; he had no expression on his face. He had no relationship to what he had done at all; he just said, 'I know I must have done it, because I'm in jail.'"

Reiner prefers not to allow actors to see their dailies, because it might hinder their performances, so Bates had to wait until the film was edited to see the results of her work. Her initial response was apprehensive, but now she's pleased with the final product. "I like the look of Annie that we got—she's like this huge, demented child," Bates offers. "She looked really out of control, like she should be back in the playpen and she somehow got out. I kept thinking, 'What is this thing I've created?' because I come from the stage and I have a real sense of what I do every night. There's a sense of completion and I know what it looks like. So it made me nervous, because here I was creating something that would last and be permanent, yet I had no idea what it was going to look like."

Working on the film did prove to be taxing—not only from the demands of keeping the intensity of the character, but even more so in the climactic fight to the death her character has with Sheldon.

"A couple of times, early on in the shooting, I found myself getting in weird moods, and I talked to Rob about it," Bates recalls. "He said, 'You can't think about this every night, just leave it at the studio.' Towards the end, when we worked out the physical confrontation between the characters, I was very disturbed going through the experience, and also by the feeling of being on the receiving end of all that frustration and anger that Jimmy's character was feeling. I wasn't prepared for my emotional response to that anger and hostility. I burst into tears after one take. It was involuntary, but it made me mad that I cried, because everything shut down and we had to stop. I was embarrassed that I wasn't doing a professional job."

As for near misses of his own with obsessed fans, Reiner related the most to Sheldon's dilemma, since he spent many years trying to shed his image from TV's *All in the Family* by coming into his own as a director. Yet he claims that to this day, people on the street still yell "Meathead" at him.

"I've had fans send me letters that have come close to overstepping the bounds," Reiner admits. "There's not much I can do . . . I'm not the kind of guy who would get that kind of stuff. I'm not somebody people would fantasize about, like Mel Gibson or Tom Cruise. The element I was drawn to was the dilemma that every creative person has, those who are lucky enough to become successful at doing a certain thing and want to break away from that and grow and change. And that fear you have because the audience that has accepted you and loves you so much may turn away from you and be upset."

Though *Misery* was a risky endeavor for the director, whose track record was spotless, Reiner is happy he was able to pull it off and receive glowing reviews that normally don't come to a Stephen King adaptation. Most importantly, *Misery* showed yet another facet of Reiner's talent that he hopes has squelched any preconceptions of the press, who deemed him a "West Coast Woody Allen" after *When Harry Met Sally . . .* was released.

"How can I be just like Woody Allen?" Reiner exclaims. "Each of my films is different from anything Woody Allen has done. I made *Spinal Tap, Stand By Me* and this film. *When Harry Met Sally . . .* was based on my experiences. I was single. I had been married just like the character. I got a divorce and was thrown back into the dating world. I'm from New York so I set the thing in New York. Nobody is allowed to make a comedy/relationship film set in New York unless they're Woody Allen? That's not fair. Now that I've done *Misery*, I'll probably be called the 'Jewish Hitchcock' or something like that."

THE DARKMAN COMETH

BY BILL WARREN

RAIMI'S DARK HERO DONS NEW BANDAGES AS HE PLANS HIS REVENGE.

Shooting this scene draws everyone toward the bizarre, grimy set of *Darkman*, now filming in a downtown Los Angeles warehouse. People put down newspapers and stand quietly in the shadows, watching Sam Raimi direct what everyone hopes will be the movie that makes him known to people outside his loyal horror audience.

Most of his head and his hands swathed in bandages, Liam Neeson grabs a broken pipe and flails it madly about him, roaring in rage. Suddenly, he glances down at his reflection (to be filmed later, of course) in a puddle of water. He staggers back against a wall and crouches slowly downward as steam cascades whitely over his face. He sobs raggedly.

Raimi is very happy with Neeson. "The most important thing about Liam," says Raimi, "was that I believed him as a real person. The toughest job that the actor had to pull off was to be a real human being in the beginning, one who was warm and believable, not too corny or phony. Liam had that particular charm, and he has pulled it off. He's just splendid."

Darkman's story is sensational, incredible—it's both familiar *and* new. The characters include some absolutely wonderful villains, the leader of which is Durant (played by Larry Drake), who snips off his victims' fingers with a gold cigar trimmer. He doesn't let those fingers go to waste, either.

Liam Neeson plays Peyton Westlake, a nice-guy scientist in love with ambitious corporate attorney Julie Hastings (Frances McDormand). While Peyton is struggling to

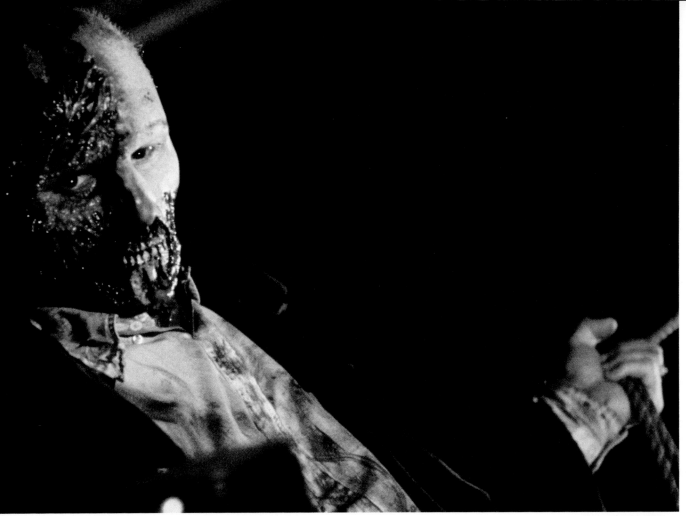

All *Darkman* photos © Universal

HIS RAVAGED FACE
FINALLY EXPOSED,
DARKMAN HOLDS
ON FOR DEAR LIFE.

create a kind of synthetic flesh (shades of *Doctor X*) that can replace tissue lost by burns or accidents, Julie is doing her best for Louis Strack (Colin Friels), a corporate developer in this unnamed American city. But in short order, Durant and his mixed bag of a gang confront a surprised Peyton in his lab. They get what they want, but the vicious Durant has Peyton tortured and disfigured, then left to die in his lab, set to blow up with a dippy-bird trigger.

Peyton, however, survives the explosion—but everyone thinks he's dead. Now hideously scarred, he makes a new lab in an abandoned soap factory and continues with his research on synthetic flesh. Only now he has a new goal: revenge. He's now Darkman, a cloaked, crimefighting avenger. And he uses his synthetic flesh to make perfect masks of Durant and his men, turning them against one another. Wearing a mask of his original face, Peyton/Darkman tries to renew his relationship with Julie, only to find that she's on the verge of falling in love with Strack.

Darkman was adapted from Raimi's original story by a whole carload of writers—Sam himself, his brother Ivan, Joshua and Daniel Goldin and Chuck Pfarrer. But the story is consistent and authentic, having no evidence of being written by different people. As you can see, however, the story does have the feeling of having been made from *other* stories—there are touches of *Phantom of the Opera*, a fragment of *Hunchback of Notre Dame*, elements of *Batman*, even terrific shards of great and pulp heroes such as The Shadow.

"It has a lot of elements from a lot of pictures that have gone before, that's for sure," admits Raimi. "The idea didn't actually come from those, though. It came from the idea of a man who can change his face to become other people. It was originally a short story I wrote, and it was accepted with encouragement by friends. It segued into a longer story, then a 40-page treatment, and then it became a story of a man who'd lost his face and *had* to take on other faces. Then it became the story of a man who battled criminals using this power. And then, because he lost his face, the idea of what would happen if he'd had a relationship *before* became important." So Raimi slowly backed into the similarities with earlier works.

The fantastic set in the abandoned warehouse is Darkman's second lab, after the explosion and fire. It's gigantic and red-lit, with sawdust on the floors, steam escaping from vents here and there and fire raging in the background. It looks positively Germanic, like something Fritz Lang would have filmed, with pillars, shattered concrete and rusty iron bars. There are two levels, with Darkman's actual lab stuff upstairs on a broken cement platform. There are upended old Sparkletts water bottles with flesh-colored solutions in them dangling from the ceiling. There are empty Chinese food cartons scattered on the junky-looking tabletop, Zagnut bars everywhere ("Darkman likes candy bars," Raimi notes), cobbled-together computers and a dusty cylinder where he generates holographic images of what he intends to create in synthetic flesh.

Production designer Randy Ser has created something that ranks among the greatest lab sets in movie history, and this writer has seen a *lot* of lab sets. This one is not a gleaming, tidy scientific research institution; it's the kind of thing jury-rigged by a brilliant, desperate man who's on the verge of losing his marbles. It matches the persona and character of Darkman perfectly.

Aside from Neeson, who merely has to *play* Darkman, the guys most responsible for the character are makeup FX creators Tony Gardner and Larry Hamlin. "Sam had a paragraph in the script that described what the Darkman was, and that was it," Gardner recalls. "I took it upon myself to sculpt my interpretation of that paragraph, and I

LARRY DRAKE SHOWS FRANCES MCDORMAND THAT HIS *L.A. Law* NICE GUY IS JUST AN ACT.

brought it into one of our meetings when we were first speaking with him. Sam and Rob were so excited, Sam wanted to keep the sculpture there; he was like, 'This is it, this is exactly how I saw it.' Knowing Sam and knowing how visually oriented he is, and knowing how things are a little more extreme than the rest of the world, I took it just a bit further in areas I thought could be gotten away with. And I think we hit a real nice balance. We've got the humanity of it and we've got the monster side too.

"The toughest challenge was the character," the makeup pro continues. "You have to sympathize with him as a human being and for what he's gone through. At the same time he plays the opposite extreme, a real nightmare-image monster to a couple of people, and he hits every variable in between, so it really had to be worked out in the very beginning steps, the sculpture and original design. I sculpted it with my key guy on the show, Chet Zar."

Raimi is well-known for his flamboyant, energetic and unique style of direction and photography. Now, he says, "The style is very different in this picture. My main goal in this film is to create real characters in something of a fantastic situation. I'm trying to keep the camera movement to a more realistic level, as opposed to a wild level, where I take on the point of view of spirits or supernatural things. I'm trying not

LEFT BELOW
PEYTON WESTLAKE'S TORTUROUS "DEATH" IS AS SHOCKING AS ANY OF THE VENGEANCE HE METES OUT LATER.

RIGHT BELOW NOT YOUR TYPICAL ROMANTIC MOMENT.

to throw the audience out of it, to have them say, 'That's a neat shot.' I'd rather they were sucked into the story and not pulled away from it. I'm trying to restrain myself."

But a scaled-down Sam Raimi is still Sam Raimi, after all, and he may be the *only* person connected with the film who thinks he's backed off a lot. Raimi's style even affected Gardner's job. "Sam doesn't really shoot with a master shot all the time for coverage," Gardner relates. "Usually when you take in the makeup, you want the close-up shot first, while the makeup's still good, and that never happens. They shoot the master and work their way down to the close-up. With Sam, the close-ups can be done any time. Darkman will be walking down some stairs with the camera following, and all of a sudden the camera will zoom in and stop inches in front of his face, with you not knowing that that shot's coming until 10 minutes before he's going to shoot it. It definitely keeps you on your toes, but the visual style is beautiful."

"Sam Raimi is an extremely talented filmmaker," asserts *Darkman* storyboardist Pete Von Sholly, "very imaginative, very clear in his vision of what he wants to see, and he also knows lenses and how to operate a camera. He has hands-on knowledge of how most things are done, which helps him to know what he can and can't do. There are several different cameras that he has invented—the Sam-o-cam, the Ram-o-cam, the Vas-o-cam." *Sure* you've toned down, Sam.

In addition to just keeping up with Raimi, Gardner had to design one of the toughest of all makeups—a subtraction makeup. Remember that makeup is something you *add* to a face; if a guy, like Darkman, has his flesh seared off, you can't very well remove the actor's own flesh. "Most of his face is burned away, and to do that on a person, to carve away, first you have to build up so you have something to cut into, so that meant we were building up his whole head, then gouging into it. His burned side was an appliance makeup that was, let's say, maybe an eighth of an inch thick. That meant that the human side of his face had to be twice that. And the thicker the foam gets, the more limited the mobility and facial expression.

"The only parts of Liam that show are the tip of his right ear and his eyelids. Everything else is fake. We've even built out his ears so that with no hair, everything looks proportional. When he plays Peyton Westlake, his ears are taped back so that they look very flat to his head. When he plays Darkman, his ears are untaped so they're standing normal. The appliance can be built out and the front of the ear recreated so the back half is still in proportion and looks stuck to the head."

A few weeks later, your loyal correspondent heads out to another *Darkman* set, built in an airplane hangar in Van Nuys. It's a gigantic place with tiny birds fluttering around the white interior. One section has been roped off, draped in black velvet. Inside the big black cube is a panoramic photo, a huge diorama of the sky-scape behind the Strack construction. Here is where the final confrontation between Darkman and the villain will occur, a fight to the death amid the skeletal girders.

There are two high falls being shot this day, as a stuntman and stuntwoman plummet from the girders onto an airbag which itself is on a pile of collapsed cardboard boxes. The attitude of the two people doing the stunts is so casual you can fall into the mistake of believing it *is* casual, but it's a very dangerous profession. It's all over in a moment—and then you realize that you just saw someone fall 30 feet straight down. Sure, they land on something soft—but how much would it take to get *you* to do that?

Or this: a few weeks later, and we're back for the last visit to the *Darkman* shoot. This is outside in downtown Los Angeles, near those buildings that used to be called skyscrapers but which now all seem to be highrises. Three helicopters take off, two with cameras, one with actors, one guy in a Larry Drake mask, and another guy— YIPE!—hanging 20 feet *beneath* the helicopter on a rope ladder. This stuntman is playing Darkman himself. They take off with a great deal of dust and noise, and flash

DARKMAN'S MAD LAB IS PLACE OF HEROES, NOT VILLAINS.

in and out among the big glass buildings, the stuntman dangling below.

Make no mistake—this is a *big* movie. And of course, there's much more money involved. "This picture has an incredible amount of miniatures and effects," producer Tapert says, "by the Skotak brothers, the best in the business. A lot of things we were doing weren't safe to do full size—blowing guys through a roof, blowing up factories, helicopters that come crashing down into moving traffic. Some of these things they just won't let you do any more," he jokes.

Evil Dead this ain't. Those movies, however great, were small, confined stories. They appealed only to limited groups of people, and *Darkman* is an attempt to break Raimi into the mainstream. "To tell you the truth," Raimi admits a bit sadly, "I've never had a movie that's done very well. FANGORIA readers are the best supporters of the movies I make, but none of them have grossed more than $2 million at the box office, which by Hollywood standards is pitiful."

"*Darkman* is aimed at the FANGORIA audience, of course," says Tapert later. "They have been very loyal to us, and there are plenty of twists and turns, the kind of thing they like, but we do need to broaden our base. *Evil Dead II* was not a success here in America. Theatrically, it died. Videowise, it did *fairly* well." Despite foreign successes, "our pictures have *never* done that well for us here, so we've got to broaden our U.S. audience, and *Darkman* is a way to do it." Stop being a cult film-making team, this interviewer asks? "*Yes,*" Tapert replies with feeling.

THE REST OF THE ADDAMS FAMILY

BY IAN SPELLING

EVEN BEFORE MAKEUP, CAREL STRUYCKEN WAS A DEAD RINGER FOR LURCH.

Though the adventures of Morticia and Gomez helped make *The Addams Family* a $100-million blockbuster, it took the rest of the macabre clan—Wednesday, Pugsley, Lurch, Thing, Cousin It, Uncle Fester and Granny—to transform the film into a family affair. And make no mistake about it—for all the lunacy and dark humor of the story, as well as the delightful romantic chemistry between Raul Julia and Anjelica Huston, much of the credit for the film's immense appeal and financial success must go directly to the family that made up the supporting cast.

"When my agent first called, she said, 'I've got another crazy thing for you,' " recalls John Franklin, who for five months donned 35 pounds of extraordinarily hot and hairy costume to become Cousin It. "I almost didn't go in for it. Then they said, 'It's Anjelica Huston, Raul Julia and Christopher Lloyd.' So I said, 'When do I start?' I loved the series; it was on when I was growing up in Chicago. I'd done the young Beast [for a flashback sequence] in TV's *Beauty and the Beast* and a Vulcan [in a video game commercial], so I'd done makeup roles. I told the casting people I really knew what I was getting myself into."

Cousin It, of course, was an innovation of the television series, not a part of the original Charles Addams comic strip canon. "I'm still trying to find him in any of the comics, but I haven't yet. I created his voice, his walk and I got to drive a car," laughs Franklin, whom fright fans may remember from 1984's *Children of the Corn*. By the end of *The Addams Family*, he even gets a girl, Margaret (Dana Ivey). "I think It is a very understanding guy. He's human, but only his family can understand him. He relates to women as people. Margaret is going through a hard time, and It is there to provide a warm, fuzzy shoulder to cry on."

Christopher Hart knew he might be the real Thing, and he was thrilled that the living hand, played by Ted (Lurch) Cassidy in the television series, would be freed from his box. "They wanted a hand with a lot of personality and a distinct look to it," Hart recalls. "They looked at several people who used their hands in their work. I happen to be a magician, so I have a lot of skill and dexterity. Once I went in and they saw I had that quality they were looking for, they wanted to see my hand look happy, sad and nervous, and walk different ways. I was up against a lot of magicians and I beat them out. I got a call back against some mimes and puppeteers, and finally got the role."

Hart, who spent much of the filming strapped to a dolly while his fingers literally did the walking, gave his all for the strenuous role. "I wanted Thing to have a real animated cartoon-type look. People seem to like what I did. They tell me they've grown to love Thing as a cute little personality, almost like a family pet. The special effects work is so well done, your disbelief is completely suspended and you just accept this hand as movie magic."

For the *Addams Family* follow-up, Hart expects moviegoers will be introduced to a lady Thing. "They had a female hand in several scenes of the television series," reveals Hart. "We actually added a female Thing to a few scenes in the movie, but it just didn't work into this particular version, so they took it back out. Maybe we'll do it in the sequel."

Carel Struycken, a veteran of *Star Trek: The Next Generation* and David Lynch's *Twin Peaks, was* Lurch. At 7 feet tall, with large, striking features and a great, angular face, Struycken encountered few difficulties becoming the character. "I think they were very smart," he comments in his thick Dutch accent. "They gave me the shape of my head with a wig. There were no prosthetics there. They tried rubber early on, but after a few days they totally got rid of it. I only had a different skin color. They just accentuated what was already there. The only thing I insisted on was that they make

All Addams' Family photos © Paramount

WEDNESDAY
(CHRISTINA RICCI)
PREPARES TO LIGHT
UP PUGSLEY'S LIFE.

me look ancient—Lurch may be 100 or 200 years old—and I got them to make my eyes darker." After 45 minutes of applying the wig and 45 more devoted to giving him his ghostly appearance, the transformation was complete.

For Struycken, the highlight of the whole experience was viewing the final product, which he caught in a packed Manhattan theater a day before facing the international press gathered in town to discuss the film. "I really enjoyed it," he enthuses. "It was nice to finally see all of the elements come together; it was really as much a surprise for us as it was for everyone else."

Famed New York stage actress Judith Malina, the widow of teacher/actor Julian (*Poltergeist II*) Beck, also found the *Addams Family* shoot a great experience. She enjoyed playing everybody's favorite kooky Granny for several reasons: One, it was a fun, over-the-top role; two, she and Struycken struck up a warm friendship; and three, Malina got to work again with Huston, with whom she co-starred in *Enemies, A Love Story*. "Making a comedy, everybody's romping and up on the funny part of it," Malina notes. "Everybody's cheerful. We shot the movie during the Gulf War, and during that time of fear and divided feelings, our shooting the film somehow added to the fact of this family, a solidarity in a world of horror creating its own world of horror.

"We had a good time together," she asserts. "One of the beauties of this movie is that these people represent our own infantile mischievousness, our own tendency to naughtiness, which we've all had to repress. We have a social contract not to do things like that, and it's a delight to see it unrepressed. Everybody has a little *Addams Family* naughtiness in them. That's why we like them so much, even though they're so bad."

WEDNESDAY AND PUGSLEY ENGAGE IN A LITTLE SWORDPLAY.

Those familiar with The Living Theater—a 45-year-old, risk-taking acting group Malina founded with Beck—may have been surprised to see the actress in so mainstream a production as *The Addams Family.* "Nobody can support a company in this [economic] situation," she explains. "It's impossible to run an art theater in the U.S., except by touring Europe or making movies. So, if making movies can help sustain The Living Theater, that's as good a way as any. I'm glad to do it and I have a good time doing it. I don't consider it a contradiction. I just find it's a way to support the art. That's what I learned from Julian doing *The Cotton Club* and *Poltergeist II.*"

Perhaps the most perfectly cast Addams is the precocious Christina Ricci, who had stolen the show from both Cher and Winona Ryder in the drama *Mermaids.* As Wednesday, Ricci utters many of the film's best lines and brings a palpable creepiness to the character of the Addams daughter. During the long shoot, the 11-year-old actress apparently kept everyone on their toes and up to date.

"Christina was always the source of information about what was happening on the set," smiles Struycken. "If we needed to know what was next or if there were going to be any changes, we'd go to Christina instead of an assistant director."

"It's true," Malina remarks. "Christina always asked intelligent questions to keep herself informed. She knows what's important."

Ricci's mother told director Barry Sonnenfeld that somewhere in the air between New York and Los Angeles, her daughter became Wednesday Friday Addams. "The first day on the set with Christina, we did a couple of takes and I didn't think Christina looked sad enough," recalls Sonnenfeld. "I went up to her and said, 'That was really good, but I want you to look a little sadder.' I started to walk away and Christina said, 'Barry,' and I said, 'Yeah, Christina.' She said, 'Sadness is an emotion and Wednesday has no emotions.'

"So I said, 'You know, Christina, you're right. Why don't you just play it a little more morose.' She said, 'Oh, OK.' To this very day I don't know what went on there. Does she know what morose means? I suspect so. Was she humoring me? I suspect so. Whatever the case, she was great."

During this interview, Ricci and Jimmy Workman, who portrayed Pugsley, sit together. Rumor had it he had a bit of a crush on her during the shoot, but no one brings the issue up. Workman is a loud, cheerful kid who likes to joke around; Ricci is ever the pro, serious and thoughtful. Asked if they got along well, they simultaneously groan, "Mmmmmm." Then the diplomatic Ricci adds, "We were a lot like brother and sister. We fought a lot and got along a lot."

The children were very impressed by fellow cast members Julia, Huston and Christopher Lloyd. "They're great," says Workman. "Really nice," Ricci concurs. "Christopher Lloyd is really shy, but once you start talking with him, he's really nice." And what about the imposing Struycken? "The first thing I thought of him was 'Whoooa!' " exclaims Workman. "Carel, he's a nice guy. He's about three of me." And despite all the hijinks the script called for—like the mock-bloody sword fight—and the broad sets, costumes and characterizations, Ricci says she had no problems taking her work seriously. "I don't remember trying to keep a straight face," she explains. "When you're really in character, you don't get out of it that quickly."

Ricci pauses for a moment when asked to select her favorite part of the *Addams Family* process. "I think watching it when it was finished," she decides. "I wasn't surprised when I saw *Mermaids.* I thought it was going to be like when we were shooting. That didn't have a lot of effects that had to be put in afterwards. Also, in *The Addams Family*, the way they used the music made a lot of the movie."

ONLY LURCH COULD STOMACH THE LEMONADE THAT THE ADDAMS KIDS BREW UP.

SINCE THING WASN'T UP FOR A GAME OF TWISTER, LURCH AND PUGSLEY CATCH A FEW WINKS.

Hart sees the sequel, *Addams Family Values*, as an opportunity to explore the characters in the supporting cast further than before. "We've just barely touched the people, just kind of established them and the look and the sets," Hart says. "It'll take a sequel to really get into the other characters."

THE "ALIEN" CHRONICLES

BY DOUGLAS E. WINTER

utside, in the light of day, the '70s were ending with a whimper; but in the darkness of our movie theaters, there was nothing but a scream. The films of a new and peculiarly American horror—notably Wes Craven's *The Hills Have Eyes*, John Carpenter's *Halloween*, George A. Romero's *Dawn of the Dead* and Sean Cunningham's *Friday the 13th*—unleashed an awesome violence upon family and fellowship. They turned the silver screen into a savage mirror of a society under siege: America in the aftermath of Watergate and Vietnam, Love Canal and Three Mile Island, recession and energy crisis and racial strife—an America whose citizens were held hostage in foreign lands and their own neighborhoods. The most popular, if not the best, of these films was Ridley Scott's 1979 shocker *Alien*.

Scripted by Dan O'Bannon and Ronald Shusett (with rewrites by producers David Giler and Walter Hill), *Alien* turned the safe and scienceless fiction of *Star Wars* and *Close Encounters of the Third Kind* two years earlier into the nation's urgent need for fear. From its opening title sequence—a view of deep space slowly pierced by a monolithic "I"—to the white-lit womb in which its sleeping crew waits, *Alien* crosses from the hopeful finale of *2001: A Space Odyssey* (1968) into a future that is terror incarnate. The result was a bona fide summer sensation whose stylish surface overwhelms its meager substance.

Seven crewmen and a cat inhabit the *Nostromo*, an impossible spaceship that is in fact a Gothic ruin—a haunted castle complete with shadowed corridors and secret passages, dripping water and rattling chains. The ship's name, taken from Joseph Conrad's sprawling novel of political corruption and revolution in South America, tips the moviemakers' hand. Conrad's *Nostromo*, like *Heart of Darkness*, is a stunning indictment of colonialism, its heroes cut off from civilization, lost in a nightworld of greed and exploitation—a world where ideals fall victim to material desires and nature is relentlessly violent. Its most vital passage could well describe the outer space of *Alien*: "No intelligence could penetrate the darkness of the Placid Gulf." Space, we quickly learn, is not the great frontier, but a third world country to be stripped and enslaved. The spaceship *Nostromo* is a mining vessel, and both its crew and the shadowy Company that owns it have no apparent god but the almighty dollar.

The crew is extraordinarily ordinary, an ensemble of non-stars and character actors, including Tom Skerritt, Harry Dean Stanton and, of course, Sigourney Weaver, who made her starring debut as Warrant Officer Ripley. Foreshadowed in the O'Bannon-scripted *Dark Star* (1974), they are not the heroic rocket jockeys of '50s space opera but a mundane, blue-collar complement whose concerns are mostly grumbling, food and getting paid. These are the men and women who built the Pinto, and Scott strongly underscores their incompetence as if to suggest that they might well deserve to die.

When the master computer, MU/TH/UR 6000 (known, inevitably, as "Mother"), detects a distress signal on unexplored planet LV-426, the *Nostromo*'s rescue mission unveils the wreckage of an alien spacecraft. At its helm is a remarkable corpse—"Bones bent outward, like it exploded from the inside"—and in its cavernous belly lies a payload of monstrous eggs. The inquisitive second officer (John Hurt, suitably named Kane) opens one of them, a literal jack-in-the-box that impregnates him with an alien lifeform, which soon explodes outward into our world.

This story is by no means original; its precursors include two classics of science fiction, A.E. Van Vogt's novel *The Voyage of the Space Beagle* (1939) and John W. Campbell's short story "Who Goes There?" (1938), which inspired the first of *Alien*'s

All *Alien* photos © 20th Century Fox

**LEFT
AND YOU THOUGHT
THE WORM AT THE
BOTTOM OF A
TEQUILA BOTTLE
WAS BAD . . .**

**RIGHT
"CAN'T I STAY JUST A
LITTLE LONGER?"
BEGS THE FIRST
FILM'S ALIEN.**

film precedents, *The Thing from Another World* (1951). The similarity of *Alien* to Edward L. Cahn's *It! The Terror from Beyond Space* (1958) was so striking that litigation resulted (the case was settled out of court); debts are also owed to Mario Bava's *Planet of the Vampires* (1965) and Curtis Harrington's *Queen of Blood* (1966).

The obvious difference is the intensity of *Alien*'s imagery; no major-studio production since *The Exorcist* had been as wet or wild. Its singular achievement was the Alien itself; Hollywood had at last transcended the thing in the rubber suit. Sigourney Weaver notwithstanding, the true stars of *Alien* are its visual FX artists and designers—especially H.R. Giger and Carlo Rambaldi—who engineered a creature that was convincingly alive, and won the 1979 Oscar for Visual Effects.

The Alien is a walking compendium of white middle-class phobias—insect and reptile, parasite and contaminant, darkman and phallus—and worst of all, it subverts that dearest of American institutions: motherhood. It is no imaginary evil, but a terror that has burst from the midsection of our society—the suburban nightmare come true, the dark-skinned, intensely masculine intruder who has but one thought in mind: our destruction. The white men are the first to die, and the women the last, saved for a fate worse than death—underscored as the Alien's tail coils around and under the navigator Lambert (Veronica Cartwright) before the camera cuts to the sound of her prolonged screams. The *Alien* soundtrack may as well have been Public Enemy's *Fear of a Black Planet*—indeed, we learn that the monster is a would-be slave that the Company is determined to bring back at all costs. And as with Romero's zombies, forget the green cards; there is no hope of integration, just a simple truth: Die, you bastard!

The humans are helpless—not simply ineffective, but utterly incapable of responding to the Alien threat. There is no semblance of control: A broken chain of command allows the Alien onboard, and when danger erupts, the soft-spoken Jimmy Carter of a captain, Dallas (Skerritt), devises a plan that leads straight to his death. Without him, the crew responds in panic, embracing the impulse to be divided and conquered that is endemic in contemporary American horror. One by one, they walk right into the Alien's waiting arms.

Their one supposed advantage—technology—cannot save them. It is no simple irony that the *Nostromo*'s science officer (Ian Holm) should prove to be a defective robot. The *Nostromo* may be capable of flight across galaxies, but nothing on board seems to work; it cannot even light its interiors. Science has not failed the crew; it has rendered them irrelevant, expendable.

When, in the film's closing moments, Ripley cries out to MU/TH/UR to halt the detonation sequence, the computer simply counts on: for science, like the Alien, is a creature "unclouded by conscience, remorse or delusions of morality." With words that have become the battlecry of the series, Ripley shouts: "You bitch!" It is a rebellion against the new mother, technology—the false promises of the television screen, the microchip, the nuclear age . . . and above all, technology's favorite bedtime story, science fiction. This is indeed a cinema of betrayal; Scott, like Joseph Conrad, warns that the pursuit of the material creates a justice founded on expediency; it is inhuman, and it is fatal.

Unfortunately, Scott's direction is uneven, particularly in the laborious opening act; later, when the bodies begin to pile up, scenes of delicious tension give way to scenes of utter stupidity. Scott simply cheats too often—as in masking the android's identity—and seems incapable of creating more than a hi-tech funhouse.

The viewer is left with a crushing sense of futility. For Ripley, there is no hope save that of escape: The umbilicus must be cut, and the mothership and its precious payload—of wealth and alien perfection—destroyed. Still the monster pursues her, and

it is here that *Alien* sheds its already flimsy skin and slips on its Halloween mask, reducing the fiercely independent Ripley first to a sentimental gesture—rescuing Jonesy the cat at the risk of her own life—and then to her underwear in a gratuitous finale. One can only wonder why Scott did not manage to work in a shower scene.

The overwhelming box-office success of *Alien* spawned a menagerie of imitators, including *Galaxy of Terror*, TV's *The Intruder Within*, *Forbidden World*, *Horror Planet*, *Xtro*, *The Being* and *Creature*—as well as John Carpenter's exquisite revisiting of *The Thing*. Not until 1986 was an official sequel released, and the wait proved worthwhile: *Aliens* is that rarest of cinematic gems, a sequel that both holds true to and surpasses its source.

The credit is due principally to director James Cameron, chosen by the original producers—Gordon Carroll, Giler and Hill—based on his high-velocity script and direction of *The Terminator*. (*Galaxy of Terror*, on which Cameron worked as a designer, was not mentioned in the publicity.) *Aliens* was written by Cameron, from a story by him, Giler and Hill, as an up-budget take on the template of its predecessor; but Cameron, the master of methedrine moviemaking, pushed the fast-forward and cranks up the volume. The result is a manic delight. Even its lapses of logic, science and common sense—and there are many—are lost in the mad rush. On every level (save James Horner's overbearing score, which pales before the music of Jerry Goldsmith in the first film), *Aliens* is a superior and more satisfying film.

Like the original, it opens in deep space, where Ripley's escape shuttle is discovered 57 years after the *Nostromo*'s destruction. Ripley is roused from hypersleep to learn that the nightmare has only begun. Over the intervening years, LV-426 has been terraformed and colonized by miners and their families . . . and the cycle is set to begin again. Communication with LV-426 is suddenly cut off, and Ripley joins another rescue mission, but this one is armed and dangerous. The humble crew of the *Nos-*

LEFT
Alien
SINGLEHANDEDLY
REDEFINED THE
LOOK OF THE
SCIENCE FICTION-
HORROR FILM.

RIGHT
RIPLEY'S INCREDIBLE
BATTLE WITH THE
QUEEN WAS
SUPPOSED TO BE
HER FINAL
ENCOUNTER WITH
THE ALIENS.

tromo is replaced by a squad of Colonial Marines, a wisecracking wild bunch of badasses who, like the S.W.A.T. team of *Dawn of the Dead*, represent that most American of beliefs: superior firepower.

With Ripley and a smarmy Company representative, Burke (Paul Reiser), in tow, the Marines descend into LV-426 to find another haunted castle, a landlocked *Nostromo* that is a maze of concrete and cables . . . and Aliens. There they find the colony's sole survivor: a little girl, Newt (Carrie Henn), who serves as a reminder of the series' subtext of betrayal. "My mommy always said there were no monsters—no *real* ones," Newt says. "But there *are* . . . Why do they tell little kids that?" She is Ripley's new kitten, the fragile dream of innocence that Ripley vows to protect at all costs.

For both Scott and Cameron, authority is the art of the lie; whether Mom or Dad, Big Money or Big Science, its broken promises have left us staring helplessly into the darkness of that Placid Gulf. Cameron, fresh from his script for *Rambo: First Blood Part II*, leaves the viewer with little doubt: his Marines are post-Vietnam (but pre-Desert Storm) veterans, soldiers who cannot win because the system will not let them. As Hudson (Bill Paxton) tells Burke: "Hey, maybe you haven't been keeping up on current events, but we just got our asses kicked, pal!" With an incompetent in command and no backup, the Marines revert from invaders to besieged in a matter of minutes; and *Aliens* reverts with them, embracing the body count aesthetics of the original as characters begin to fall like dominoes.

As we witness yet again the salient human urge in contemporary horror films—to be divided and conquered—it is all too apparent that these films exploit our growing fear that every social unit has broken down: friendship, the family, the team, the neighborhood, the school, the corporation, the Army, the government . . . all of them fail. It is left to the individual to pick up the pieces, and Ripley, unlike the better-trained and better-armed soldiers, survives not due to her compassion or humanity, but because of her fierce individuality. She has indeed been alienated, and this aloneness—this essential *oneness*—is her saving grace.

Cameron elicits captivating performances from his cast, notably Michael Biehn as the tough but sensitive Corporal Hicks, the irrepressible Paxton as the loud-mouthed Hudson, Lance Henriksen as the "good" android Bishop—and, of course, Weaver, who received an Academy Award nomination for a role she had initially declined. But like Scott, Cameron lets Ripley's character elude him in the final act, when, in order to rescue Newt, she Rambos her way into the depths of the colony to confront the sequel's "bitch," the egg-laying Alien Queen.

The showdown between the two finds Ripley flex-dancing in robotic drag for cinema's most cataclysmic catfight. Its climax is arguably the most frightening scene of the two films, as Newt, saved from the Queen, calls Ripley "Mommy"—simultaneously rejecting her natural mother, whose sole offense was to die at the hands of the Aliens, and embracing in her place a killing machine as violent and intense as any monster. This is a peculiar moral—to defeat the enemy we must become the enemy—and a forerunner of the awkward misogyny of the 1991 hits by both Cameron (*Terminator 2*) and Scott (*Thelma & Louise*): the "new" woman as exterminating angel. With the publicity for *Alien³* invoking the inevitable punchline—"The bitch is back"—one can only wonder aloud: Which bitch?

HISTORY OF HORROR: THE 1960s

BY TIM LUCAS

The importance of the horror films of the '30s, '40s and '50s cannot be diminished, at least not where popularity is concerned. The pioneering artists behind its greasepaint and megaphones have become—indeed, immediately became—synonymous with the genre. Nevertheless, it is the horror films of the '60s which represent the maturation of the genre, and this decade is second only to the '20s in terms of its serious contribution to the history of imaginative moviemaking. The '60s were a tumultuous period that witnessed screen horror being pulled in a number of fascinating directions: the continuation and evolution of the new Gothic cinema, as spearheaded by Hammer and the Edgar Allan Poe renaissance of AIP; the resulting development of international horror cinema, and the international coproduction; the maturation of the genre, especially its concerns with psychology and eroticism, culminating in the introduction of the MPAA rating system; and finally, a preoccupation with scenarios of apocalypse, the result of a generation of young filmmakers turned cynical and bloody-minded by the first televised war and assassination in history.

This thumbnail survey cannot hope to encompass all that was part and parcel of the '60s in such limited space, so we must defer all discussion of everything ephemeral —the Mexican horror films released here by K. Gordon Murray, the Gamera cycle, and most of the hokum produced by the Amicus team—as well as everything lovably low-rent, like *The Brain That Wouldn't Die* (1962) and the early work of Paul Naschy. Ironically, after jettisoning all the flotsam and jetsam and arriving at my choices for the top 13 horror films of the '60s, I find that few titles on my list capture or represent what that decade is best remembered for.

Most of the genre luminaries of the '50s continued to make films in the '60s, but their greatest films were already behind them. After a chain of Technicolor successes in the '50s, director Terence Fisher used Hammer Films productions like *The Two Faces of Dr. Jekyll* (1961) and *Phantom of the Opera* (1962) to forge an unconventional universe where the villains were not monsters, but rather misunderstood demons of the human soul. Fisher gave these new films offbeat, sometimes metaphysical structures that proved uncommercial, and was punished by the studios he helped build with temporary expellment. Likewise, Hammer's top stars—Peter Cushing and Christopher Lee—may have stared with icy-blue or blood-red eyes off the covers of best-selling monster magazines of the period, but their mid-'60s output seldom rewarded their fans' enthusiasm. Cushing and Lee made good films in the '60s, but they had to await Fisher's return to Hammer before achieving peak form again: Lee in *The Devil Rides Out* (a.k.a. *The Devil's Bride*, 1968), and Cushing in *Frankenstein Must Be Destroyed* (1969), the latter being an underrated masterpiece that can stand beside the best of Hitchcock as an example of letter-perfect suspense.

In America, the master showman William Castle followed the success of his atypically serious chiller *Homicidal* with a series of films that, unlike his exploitation classics of the '50s, separated the laughs from the chills. As a result, his horror films (*Mr. Sardonicus, Strait-Jacket*) became as lacking in personality as his comedies (*13 Frightened Girls, The Spirit is Willing*) were devoid of humor. It was not until 1968, when Castle produced Roman Polanski's film of *Rosemary's Baby*, that he achieved the classic horror film he'd long been hankering for.

Castle's erstwhile horror star Vincent Price followed a hugely rewarding decade as the high priest of 3-D and Emergo by settling into a long and entertaining series of Edgar Allan Poe adaptations for director Roger Corman and AIP. Seeing *Pit and the Pendulum* (1962), *Tales of Terror* (1962) or the parodic *The Raven* (1963) today on home video, with their panoramic widescreen expressionism cropped and squashed and their intense Pathe color desaturated like bled fruit, it's hard to explain the thrall in which this series held a generation. Only the last two entries in the series—*The Masque of the Red Death* (1964) and *Tomb of Ligeia* (1965)—rank with the decade's greatest achievements (*Masque* misses my list only as a matter of personal preference), but with *Tales of Terror*'s "The Facts in the Case of M. Valdemar," Corman actually out-delivers George Romero's tired rendering in *Two Evil Eyes*.

If we remember Barbara Steele as the Queen of '60s Horror, it is because her debut in Mario Bava's *Black Sunday* (1960) overshadows the entire decade. She made some unquestionably fine films in its wake—Riccardo Freda's *The Horrible Dr. Hichcock* (1962) and Camillo Mastrocinque's *An Angel for Satan* (1966), to name only two—but, while these ride high on many "favorite" film lists, their impacts were not popularly felt and they cannot join the Top 13.

The success of *Black Sunday* in America led not only to Steele's abused (and denied) celebrity but, more importantly, to an escalation of horror film production all over the world. Most of the resulting films that arrived were shown in America under the banner of AIP, which, as is now becoming apparent, not only dubbed them into idiocy, but re-edited the strongest of them to dilute their uncompromising impact. AIP's softened versions of Bava's *Evil Eye* (1962) and *Black Sabbath* (1963) erased the evolution of the *giallo* (and the development of the decade's most visionary horror director) from America's view; consequently, the distribution of an untampered-with *Blood and Black Lace* (1964, by Allied Artists) came as too much of a shock for most

viewers. Among the best European films from this period were Italy's *Mill of the Stone Women* (1960), *The Ghost* (1963), *The Witch* (1966) and Bava's final Gothic master-piece, *Kill, Baby Kill!* (1966); the twisted Spanish horrotica of Jess Franco's *The Awful Dr. Orloff* (1962), *The Diabolical Dr. Z* (1966) and *Venus in Furs* (1969); and West Germany's stylish series of Edgar Wallace adaptations, particularly those directed by F.J. Gottlieb and Alfred Vohrer. In a sense, the European horror cycle of the '60s climaxed with *Spirits of the Dead* (1967), an experimental Poe anthology film directed by Roger Vadim, Louis Malle and Federico Fellini. Fellini's "Toby Dammit," a hallucinatory reinvention of Poe's haunted, drink-soaked universe, would not only have made the Top 13 as a separate, self-contained feature, it would have *topped* it.

The '60s were the best of times; they were also the worst of times. It was the decade of John Gilling (*Plague of the Zombies*) and Herschell Gordon Lewis (*2000 Maniacs!*); of Herk Harvey (*Carnival of Souls*) and Andy Milligan (*The Ghastly Ones*); of Jack Clayton (*The Innocents*) and Larry Buchanan (*Zontar, the Thing from Venus*); of Inoshiro Honda (*Attack of the Mushroom People*) and Al Adamson (*Blood of Dracula's Castle*); of Don Sharp (*Kiss of the Vampire*) and Del Tenney (*Horror of Party Beach*); of Curtis Harrington (*Games*) and David L. Hewitt (*Dr. Terror's Gallery of Horrors*); and, to acknowledge one of the field's most schizophrenic cases, Freddie Francis (*The Skull*) and Freddie Francis (*The Deadly Bees*). It was also the decade of lovably lurid shockers like *Spider Baby* and *The Flesh Eaters* (both 1963). And it was without question the finest decade for televised terror; you simply can't consider the '60s without *The Outer Limits*, *The Twilight Zone* or your local television station's *Shock Theater*.

Unfortunately, there is a great deal of '60s horror which we, in America, have yet to appraise. An entire substrata of uncommerical, intense and pathologically twisted horror films existed as long as 30 years ago in countries with filmmaking standards freer than our own commercial cinema would allow, most of them unknown to American scholars until the publication of Phil Hardy's *The Encyclopedia of Horror Movies* in 1986. Given Hardy's tantalizing descriptions, the Brazilian films of José Mojica Marins (like *Esta Noite Encarnerei no Teu Cadaver*, "Tonight I Will Make Your Corpse Turn Red," 1966), or the Japanese *Okasaretu Byuakiu* ("Violated Angels," 1967) and *Moju* ("The Blind Beast," 1969) read as if they actually embodied the holocaust at which our manacled English-language cinema could only hint. These unseen international contenders could only have made my process of elimination more impossible.

TOP 13 HORROR FILMS OF THE '60s

***The Birds* (Alfred Hitchcock, 1963):** Hitchcock's last truly classic work sets the apocalyptic tone for the decade; it denies itself a "The End" card, knowing such a statement would only be redundant.

***The Whip and the Body* (Mario Bava, 1963):** Released here in butchered form as *What!*, this frankly erotic film provides the missing link between the Gothic horror strain and the dawning psychological thriller.

***Kwaidan* (Masaki Kobayashi, 1963):** A very long film (2 hours and 41 minutes) based on selections from Lafcadio Hearn's very short book of Japanese ghost stories; this very description is itself a testament to the dominance of the film's style over its content. Delicate, exhilarating and chilling to behold, it makes Argento's work look hurried by comparison.

***The Horror Chamber of Dr. Faustus* (Georges Franju, 1959/64):** The French masterpiece *Les Yeux Sans Visage* ("Eyes Without a Face," 1959) was not seen here until this dubbed version was issued in 1964—with *The Manster*! Both versions of the film have their respective charms—of atmosphere and authenticity—and share the mastery of Franju, whose genius was to wed weightless fantasy and harsh reality to produce an overpowering frisson.

***Blood and Black Lace* (Mario Bava, 1964):** This, the most incendiary of all horror films, remains Bava's definitive work; *Black Sunday*, of course, was a lucky aberration. A ripely misogynistic approach keeps plot and character at bay, while deriving (and provoking) genuinely sadistic pleasure from a series of breathtakingly-photographed murders. The '80s couldn't have existed without it. The macabre Carlo Rustichelli score is worth everything Goblin ever recorded.

***Onibaba* (Kaneto Shindo, 1964):** Perhaps the least-known film on this list to most horror fans, this terrifying widescreen fable is similar to Michael Reeves' *Conqueror Worm* (see below) in the way it holds up the 16th century to reflect the repressive atmosphere of its own era. It conveys the dictum that "Horror is the removal of masks" better than any of the *Phantom of the Opera* films.

***Repulsion* (Roman Polanski, 1966):** For most of its running time, this classic consists of just Catherine Deneuve in an empty apartment, falling apart. Polanski made only great films in the '60s—*Knife in the Water, Cul-de-Sac, Rosemary's Baby*—but this one (made less than respectfully, according to his autobiography) remains one of the great textbook examples of horror filmmaking. The final shot—quite ordinary, when seen out of context—never fails to raise gooseflesh when viewed in summation.

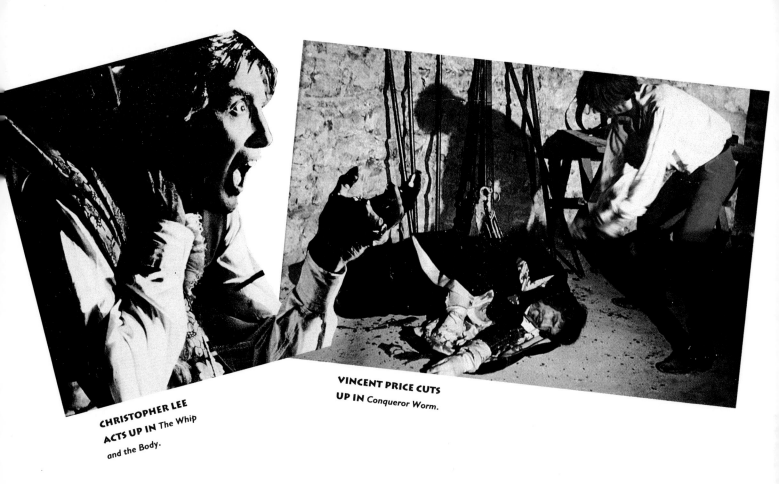

CHRISTOPHER LEE ACTS UP IN *The Whip and the Body.*

VINCENT PRICE CUTS UP IN *Conqueror Worm.*

***The Tomb of Ligeia* (Roger Corman, 1965):** Though handicapped in any number of ways—Vincent Price is too old for his role; the English scenery ignores the story's American Gothic origins; it shies away from the story's darkest implications of necrophilia and drug addiction—*Ligeia* is one of the best-written and best-looking of all horror films. Ice has been known to form on viewers' necks at Elizabeth Shepherd's pronouncement: "I will *always* be your wife!"

***Hour of the Wolf* (Ingmar Bergman, 1966):** A soft-spoken introspective psychodrama which prefigures—of all films—David Cronenberg's *The Brood* (1979), another cold-looking, chill-inducing movie about a marriage rocked to its foundations by one partner's irresistible private hell. You'll never forget the eyeball cocktail.

***Quatermass and the Pit* (Roy Ward Baker, 1967):** Known in America as *Five Million Years to Earth*, this third entry in Nigel Kneale's series of Quatermass scripts is easily the most successful and fluent of all attempts to meld horror and science fiction. SF dominates the scenario—a buried object, thought to be a World War II bomb, turns out to be a Martian spacecraft buried at a depth equal to 5 million years—until the ship "revives," reviving with it the horror of a dormant evil at the core of Man. Absolutely riveting, and one of Hammer's best films.

***Targets* (Peter Bogdanovich, 1967):** The importance of Karloff's last great film owes less to what it *is* than to what it *does*, in describing the impasse screen horror had reached in an age desensitized by everyday horrors and their constant replays. In a sense, this film is the eulogy for all the fantasy that had come before.

A DANCE OF
WITCHES IN *The
Devil's Bride.*

***Conqueror Worm* (a.k.a. *Witchfinder General*, Michael Reeves, 1968):** This film takes us back into the time and stuff of fairy tales—the 16th-century English countryside, and its witches—to illustrate, with unflinching brutality and Marlovian bravado, how distance has lent enchantment to a moral cesspool. Just as Karloff's presence lent poignance to the elegiac *Targets*, Vincent Price authorizes this milestone with his most harrowing performance. Symmetrically scripted, deeply felt (to say the least), it builds to one of the most powerful and emotionally complex finales in screen history. Reeves died of a drug overdose shortly after the film's release, intensifying its pleas for a saner world. They don't make them like this anymore; they don't let them.

***Night of the Living Dead* (George A. Romero, 1968):** Romero's debut coincided so closely with Reeves' swan song that Evil—in the form of mean-spirited, human evil —seemed to win out over Good simultaneously on two continents. This particular film is perhaps the least polished of all those composing this list, but no film better encapsulates the frustrations, the conflicts and disturbing images associated with the '60s. To watch this roughly-hewn remnant today is to be submerged in nightmarish nostalgia: The characters form a volatile cross-section of society, informed by television, and the horror described in bulletins is coming home, is already outside, banging to be let in. The walking dead in the fields are the image of gaunt, exhausted soldiers stumbling through rice paddies, and every graphic head-wound delivers the sick punch of the Dallas newsreels. Almost 10 years after *The Birds*, this film tries to soften the bitter denouement with ''The End.'' Only now, somehow, you don't buy it.

MIA FARROW BEARS
Rosemary's Baby.

HISTORY OF HORROR: THE 1970s

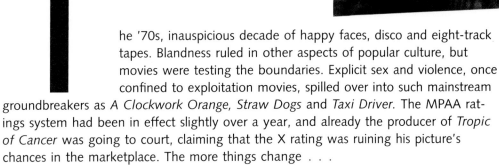

BY MAITLAND McDONAGH

The Texas Chainsaw Massacre **INTRODUCED A NEW, HUMAN MONSTER, LEATHERFACE.**

The '70s, inauspicious decade of happy faces, disco and eight-track tapes. Blandness ruled in other aspects of popular culture, but movies were testing the boundaries. Explicit sex and violence, once confined to exploitation movies, spilled over into such mainstream groundbreakers as *A Clockwork Orange, Straw Dogs* and *Taxi Driver.* The MPAA ratings system had been in effect slightly over a year, and already the producer of *Tropic of Cancer* was going to court, claiming that the X rating was ruining his picture's chances in the marketplace. The more things change . . .

Disaster movies made moviegoers afraid of luxury liners, tall buildings and the endless variety of nature's wrath, from earthquakes to killer bees. Softcore romps featuring coeds, stewardesses and nurses filled the drive-ins. Martial arts movies came to America in the form of *Five Fingers of Death,* and soon, everybody was humming "Kung Fu Fighting." It was a decade dominated by blaxploitation and biker pictures, sequels and freakish trends.

Take cannibal movies, for instance. There was everything from the historical whimsy of *How Tasty Was My Little Frenchman* (1971) to the contemporary nastiness of *Tender Flesh* (1973), directed by and starring Laurence Harvey; from comedies like *The Corpse Grinders* (1971), *Cannibal Girls* and *The Folks at Red Wolf Inn* (both 1972) and *Motel Hell* (1980) to the hi-tech *Soylent Green* and bottom-of-the-barrel *Raw Meat* (both 1973). Then there were the "Don't" films: *Don't Look Now* and *Don't Look in the Basement* (both 1973), *Don't Open the Window* (1974), *Don't Go in the House* and *Don't Answer the Phone* (both 1980). A generation of horror fans went to the movies in the shadow of a great wagging finger.

The dominance of English horror production companies—Hammer, Amicus et al.—ended in a welter of inferior cash-ins on the formulas that took the genre by storm in the late '50s and '60s. *Scars of Dracula* (1971), *Blood from the Mummy's Tomb*, *Twins of Evil* and *Hands of the Ripper* (all 1972), *Frankenstein and the Monster from Hell*, *Captain Kronos: Vampire Hunter* and *Horror Hospital* (all 1973) and *The Satanic Rites of Dracula* (1974; a.k.a. *Count Dracula and His Vampire Bride*) witnessed the death throes.

There had always been sequels, of course, and the '70s were filled with an onslaught of *Rocky*s and *Dirty Harry*s. Of course, none of them could match Sean S. Cunningham's *Friday the 13th* (1980), the movie sold all over the world before it was made. Jason hacked his way through eight further adventures, before expiring (so they promise) in 1993's *Jason Goes to Hell.*

Blaxploitation movies about fly-guys named Slaughter and Shaft and Hammer were one thing, but the race-change variants on popular hits were another. The titles included *Blacula* (1972), *Blackenstein* (1973), *Dr. Black and Mr. Hyde* and *Voodoo*

R-RATED FLICKS LIKE *Humanoids from the Deep* TESTED THE WATERS OF THE EXPLICIT GORE BEFORE THE MPAA'S CRACKDOWN IN THE 80'S.

Black Exorcist (both 1975). Even they couldn't touch some of the other hybrid genre titles for sheer ludicrous invention: witness *Werewolves on Wheels* (1971), *The 7 Brothers Meet Dracula* and *The Werewolf of Washington* (both 1973), *Sugar Hill and Her Zombie Hitmen* (1974), *Satan's Cheerleaders* (1977) and *Vampire Hookers* (1979).

1971 got off to a flying start as Roger Corman directed his last film for two decades, *Von Richthofen and Brown*. But Corman, exploitation mogul since 1954, wasn't easing out of the business—not by a long shot. Abandoning his long association with AIP, Corman founded New World Pictures and threw himself into production and distribution. Careers he helped launch in the '70s included those of directors Martin Scorsese, Jonathan Demme, Paul Bartel and Joe Dante.

Highlights of '71 included the first Amando de Ossorio *Blind Dead* movie and Clint Eastwood's debut as a writer/director with the original *Fatal Attraction*, *Play Misty for Me*, in which he plays a mellow DJ (!) with a deadly fan club of one.

Lesbian vampires turned up in Stephanie Rothman's *The Velvet Vampire* and Harry Kümel's *Daughters of Darkness*. Rothman's thoroughly modern vampire lures hippies to her desert hideaway and has her way with them (echoes of Manson's Spahn ranch add a nasty edge): Kümel's bloodsucker is the ultimate silent film star, a glittering blond goddess (the mysterious Delphine Seyrig) whose marcel-waved exterior conceals a heart of lethal ice. Both pack a powerful erotic punch, as does José Larraz's *Vampyres* (1975), featuring two sexy female blood drinkers.

IS IT SOUP YET? *The Rocky Horror Picture Show* **BECAME THE FIRST FILM IN WHICH THE AUDIENCE HAS AS MUCH DIALOGUE AS THE CHARACTERS.**

© 20th Century Fox

THE TALL MAN
REDEFINED SCREEN
MENACE IN THE
SURREALISTIC
Phantasm.

Robert Kelljan clocked in with *The Return of Count Yorga*, ringing a couple of clever changes on the vampire-in-flaky-California theme: star Robert Quarry went on to play a vampire guru in *The Deathmaster* (1972). *Night of Dark Shadows* flopped and Collinwood was banished to the land of TV reruns. Italian horror stylist Dario Argento's *The Cat O' Nine Tails* followed 1970's *The Bird With the Crystal Plumage*, and led to *Four Flies on Grey Velvet* (1974), *Deep Red* (1976) and the phantasmagoric *Suspiria* (1977) and *Inferno* (1980), the first two-thirds of his yet-uncompleted Three Mothers trilogy.

Herschell Gordon Lewis, ultraviolence pioneer, made his last film—*The Gore Gore Girls*—in 1972, but new blood waited in the wings. Wes Craven arrived with *Last House on the Left*, produced by Sean S. Cunningham. Cruel, relentless and not much fun, *Last House* attracted attention for its gritty, realistic violence, as well as Hallmark's catchy (and much imitated) "Keep Telling Yourself: It's Only a Movie . . ." ad campaign. Craven hit his stride with the gloriously mean *The Hills Have Eyes* (1977), though his subsequent career has had its ups and downs. Larry Cohen also made his directing debut in '72 with *Bone*, in which a Beverly Hills couple is terrorized by a black ex-con. Following *Black Caesar* and its sequel, *Hell Up in Harlem*, Cohen abandoned blaxploitation for such high-concept horror as *It's Alive* (1974, monster baby runs amok), *It Lives Again* (1978, *three* monster babies run amok) and *God Told Me*

To (1976, the Messiah is an alien hermaphrodite). Terminally uneven, Cohen delivered on his warped promise just often enough to keep audiences interested.

Larry Hagman directed *Beware! the Blob*, Ralph Bates and Martine Beswick starred as *Dr. Jekyll and Sister Hyde*, killer bunnies terrorized Arizona in *Night of the Lepus*, Paul Bartel explored sexual perversity in a rundown rooming house in *Private Parts* (MGM didn't release it, someone observed; it escaped) and Alfred Hitchcock made his final no-holds-barred thriller: the horrifying *Frenzy*.

1973 was the year of *The Exorcist*. Dogged by rumors of a curse on the production, William Friedkin's adaptation of William Peter Blatty's best-selling book generated controversy and major box office. Dick Smith's special FX set new standards, Mike Oldfield's "Tubular Bells" made the charts and Linda Blair set foot on the path to B-movie slutdom. Ripoffs were legion, including *Abby, Exorcism's Daughter* and *The Tempter* (all 1974), *Beyond the Door* and *House of Exorcism* (both 1975).

With several offbeat features to his credit, Brian De Palma went genre with *Sisters*, a creepy, sophisticated movie about Siamese twins. Three years later, his adaptation of Stephen King's *Carrie* catapulted him into the limelight. Body count movies were also big news. Robert Fuest's *The Abominable Dr. Phibes* (1971) and its sequel *Dr. Phibes Rises Again* (1972) perfected the outlandish mechanics, though slice-and-dice pictures really took off later, in the wake of *Friday the 13th*. Still, in '73 actor-turned-director Darren *(The Night Stalker)* McGavin's *Happy Mother's Day, Love George*, Mario Bava's *Twitch of the Death Nerve* and Douglas Hickox's *Theater of Blood* all turned serial slaughter into exercises in gory ingenuity.

Other events of note: Nicholas *(Time After Time)* Meyer wrote *Invasion of the Bee Girls*, Tab Hunter starred in the sleazy *Arousers*, Corman's *Little Shop of Horrors* was remade as the softcore *Please Don't Eat My Mother!* and George Romero directed the underrated *Crazies*. Romero's contributions to the decade also included *Martin* (1977) and the seminal zombie gutcruncher *Dawn of the Dead* (1979). Finally, John Hayes provided one nasty little picture, the underrated *Grave of the Vampire.*

John Carpenter, Tobe Hooper and Oliver Stone were the new faces of 1974. Stone made *Seizure*, a complex rubber reality picture starring Jonathan Frid and Martine Beswick; when mainstream respectability beckoned, he took it off his résumé and tried to claim *The Hand* (1981) as his first film. Carpenter unveiled the SF spoof *Dark Star*; he hit the jackpot four years later with *Halloween*. Hooper burst onto the scene with *The Texas Chainsaw Massacre*, the meat movie that wouldn't quit. Having started at the top, there was nowhere for Hooper to go but down, which he did, starting with *Eaten Alive* (1976).

Bob *(Porky's)* Clark had three good horror movies in release: *Deathdream* (Tom Savini's first credit), a monkey's paw variant with a Vietnam twist; *Deranged*, an Ed Gein-inspired movie; and *Black Christmas*, the seminal "they've-traced-the-calls-and-they're-coming-from-inside-the-house" thriller. What went wrong with Clark after that is anyone's guess. Paul Morrissey directed *Andy Warhol's Frankenstein* and *Andy Warhol's Dracula*, both featuring wan Udo Kier and buckets of blood.

In 1975, the most popular horror spoof of all time made the transition from stage to screen. *The Rocky Horror Picture Show* appealed to alienated adolescents everywhere with its exhortation to live out your wildest dreams in tacky monster movie terms. Following star Tim Curry's lead, Christopher Lee wore a dress in the subtle *The Wicker Man*, written by Anthony Shaffer, while Steven Spielberg made hydrophobia fashionable with *Jaws* and Peter Fonda and Warren Oates tried to outrun satanists in *Race with the Devil*. All in all, a mild year.

1976 took care of that with two gross-out shockfests: *The Incredible Torture Show* (later rereleased as *Bloodsucking Freaks*) and *Snuff*. Joel M. Reed's *TITS* strung together mean-spirited scenes of torture and murder to no end, while *Snuff* was a Manson picture with a tacked-on ending (by distributor Alan Shackleton) designed to cash in on the snuff movie scandal.

The first of three *Omen* films (*Damien—Omen II* followed in 1978, and *The Final Conflict* in 1981) debuted in 1976, but the high point of the year was certainly David Cronenberg's *They Came From Within* (a.k.a. *Shivers*). His first feature laid out all the themes and images that continue to obsess Cronenberg, and the genre would be immeasurably poorer without *Rabid* (1977), *The Brood* (1979) and the rest of his unique output. Peter Weir's *The Cars That Ate Paris* (a.k.a. *The Cars That Eat People*) made a smaller splash, but cleared the way for such eerie thrillers as *Picnic at Hanging Rock* (1977) and *The Last Wave* (1978).

David Bowie was an alien in Nicolas Roeg's *The Man Who Fell to Earth*, killer worms rampaged in *Squirm* and Charles Band remade (badly) George Franju's *Les Yeux Sans Visage* as *Mansion of the Doomed*.

Nobody knew what to make of it then, and nobody really knows what to make of it now, but David Lynch's first film, *Eraserhead*, was the talk of 1977. Otherwise, things were quiet on the genre front, except down in Florida, where amphibious Nazis terrorized Peter Cushing and Brooke Adams in Ken Wiederhorn's *Shock Waves*. *The Incredible Melting Man* showcased Rick Baker's disgusting melting FX in a sort-of remake of *First Man Into Space* crossed with *The Creeping Unknown*, and Julie Christie was raped by a computer in Donald Cammell's *Demon Seed*.

Big-budget spectaculars and low-budget horror shows jostled for space in 1978. The former included *The Eyes of Laura Mars*, *Coma*, *The Fury*, *Magic*, *The Boys from Brazil* and Philip Kaufman's remake of *Invasion of the Body Snatchers*. Holding up the gutter end were *The Toolbox Murders*, with Cameron Mitchell as a murderous handyman; *Alice, Sweet Alice*, in which a very young Brooke Shields is murdered on the day of her first communion; *Dracula's Dog*, another Band flick; *Blue Sunshine*, a prescient "Just Say No" opus about LSD with scary side effects; and the notorious rape/revenge shocker *I Spit on Your Grave*, originally (and disingenuously) titled *Day of the Woman*.

1979 was a landmark year. Ridley Scott took monster-in-the-house conventions from the year one and gave them new life in his much-imitated but never-equalled *Alien*. H.R. Giger and Carlo Rambaldi's alien redefined the look of the BEM, and *Alien* ripoffs proliferated in the '80s. *The Amityville Horror* introduced that troubled Long Island abode, and Don Coscarelli's *Phantasm* gave life to the Tall Man, undertaker from hell. Pallid Carol Kane was tormented in *When a Stranger Calls*, a knockout reworking of the classic babysitter tale (they've-traced-the-calls . . .). Abel Ferrara directed and starred in *Driller Killer* and Frank Langella toplined John Badham's lavish but DOA remake of *Dracula*. German director Werner Herzog went back to the silent era for inspiration and cast Klaus Kinski in his remake of *Nosferatu*. Again, production values reigned supreme and chills were lacking.

1980's contribution to vampire lore: *Dracula Sucks*. Also that year, *Without Warning* tested out the idea that got the big-budget treatment in *Predator*, Mel Gibson secured his position as postapocalyptic heartthrob in *Mad Max*, Kinski starred as a California shrink (!) in *Schizoid*, radioactive tots with black fingernails killed their parents in *The Children* and underwater monsters raped unwary women in *Humanoids from the Deep*, when Jim met Gale Anne . . .

The decade came to a close in 1980 with the promise of still more explicit horrors to come; witness William Lustig's *Maniac* (released with a self-imposed X) and Lucio Fulci's cannibal gorefest *Zombie*. "We Are Going to Eat You," the posters swore. And they did.

© Laurel

GEORGE ROMERO MADE HIS ZOMBIES EVEN MORE SHOCKING IN COLOR WITH THE CLASSIC *Dawn of the Dead.*

TOP 13 HORROR FILMS OF THE '70s

Don't Look Now (1973)
Grave of the Vampire (1973)
The Texas Chainsaw Massacre (1974)
Deathdream (1974)
Deep Red (1976)
They Came from Within (1976)
The Hills Have Eyes (1977)
Eraserhead (1977)
Martin (1977)
Halloween (1978)
The Last Wave (1978)
Alien (1979)
Phantasm (1979)

HISTORY OF HORROR: THE 1980s

BY MICHAEL GINGOLD

© 20th Century Fox

By 1981, the only two-year-old slasher film trend was already starting to show signs of wear and tear. Nearly every major and independent distributor had released a stalker movie the previous year, and with the exception of Paramount's *Friday the 13th* and Avco Embassy's *Prom Night*, none had done well at the box office. The losers included *Terror Train*, *He Knows You're Alone*, *New Year's Evil*, *Graduation Day* and various others centered around holidays and high schools. Horror had started to lose some of the respectability and acceptance it had achieved in the late '70s; now, critics charged, the genre had become an excuse for the misogynistic ripping apart of young women. Producers quickly moved out of the slasher field to concentrate on other kinds of terror.

It was only after slasher movies ceased to exist as a trend that the possibility for quality examples became apparent. Late 1982 saw the release of Jack Sholder's *Alone in the Dark*, which blended a multiple maniac plotline with dark satire to outshine all the other *Halloween* ripoffs. The latter half of the decade gave us such superior titles as Robert Harmon's stark *The Hitcher*, Joseph Ruben's diabolical *The Stepfather* and Philip Noyce's stylish *Dead Calm*; Adrian Lyne's *Fatal Attraction*, a glossy thriller with the heart of a slasher flick, was one of the top-grossing films of 1987. Then, in 1989, John McNaughton's three-year-old *Henry: Portrait of a Serial Killer* became a cause célèbre among the horror community; when it achieved theatrical release in 1990, it garnered the best reviews of any genre film in recent memory.

A few of the most popular slashers from previous decades were subjected to sequelization in the '80s. *Psycho II* and *III* turned out better than expected, with

DAVID CRONENBERG'S HUMANISTIC APPROACH TO HORROR FINALLY FOUND A MASS AUDIENCE WITH *The Fly.*

intelligent direction by (respectively) Richard Franklin and Anthony Perkins. The long string of *Friday the 13th* sequels, on the other hand, depended on the same plot every time, substituting cheap gimmicks for story creativity. And those who complained about the Michael Myers-less *Halloween III* got just what they deserved when Moustapha Akkad produced the needless (and largely worthless) *Halloween 4* and *5*.

While the stalker film was having its ups and downs, filmmakers working with other types of horror started to push the envelope of onscreen violence. Tom Savini's groundbreaking work in *Dawn of the Dead* and *Friday the 13th* was the spearhead of a new intensity in graphic special FX. Rick Baker won the first competitive Oscar for makeup with John Landis' *An American Werewolf in London*; Rob Bottin, a Baker protégé, created the gruesome monster FX for John Carpenter's remake of *The Thing*, work that many feel has yet to be equalled. Most recently, Chuck Russell's remake of *The Blob* combined the talents of Lyle Conway and Tony Gardner for a super monsterfest. Other artists parlayed FX "stardom" into directing jobs, including Stan Winston (*Pumpkinhead*), Chris Walas (*The Fly II*) and Savini himself (the remake of *Night of the Living Dead*).

Over on the independent side, the success of *Dawn of the Dead*'s unrated release inspired a string of movies to use the same self-imposed "No one under 17 admitted" slogan. These titles ranged from homegrown product like *Maniac* and *Mother's Day* to

© Lorimar TV

TV HORROR WAS BIG IN THE '80S TOO, THOUGH ON THE TUBE, *Freddy's Nightmares* DIDN'T QUITE CUT IT.

© Universal

THE '80S SAW MONSTER MAKEUP GAIN ACADEMY AWARD RESPECT, STARTING WITH *An American Werewolf in London*.

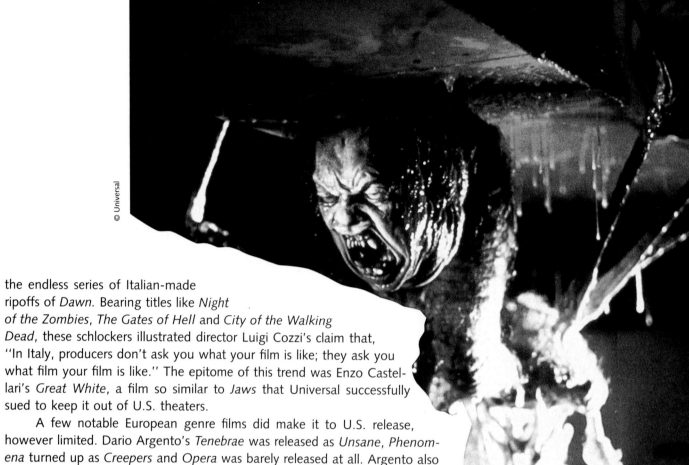
© Universal

the endless series of Italian-made
ripoffs of *Dawn*. Bearing titles like *Night
of the Zombies*, *The Gates of Hell* and *City of the Walking
Dead*, these schlockers illustrated director Luigi Cozzi's claim that,
"In Italy, producers don't ask you what your film is like; they ask you
what film your film is like." The epitome of this trend was Enzo Castel-
lari's *Great White*, a film so similar to *Jaws* that Universal successfully
sued to keep it out of U.S. theaters.

A few notable European genre films did make it to U.S. release,
however limited. Dario Argento's *Tenebrae* was released as *Unsane*, *Phenom-
ena* turned up as *Creepers* and *Opera* was barely released at all. Argento also
popped up as the producer of Lamberto Bava's energetic gorefest *Demons* and
its lackluster sequel. Taking these films' horror-movies-become-reality motifs
to a more intellectual level, Spanish director Bigas Luna gave us *Anguish*; down in
Mexico, long-absent cult filmmaker Alejandro Jodorowsky made the bizarre and disturbing *Santa Sangre*.

The Thing **WAS THE DECADE'S FX SHOW-CASE.**

Britain also exported a few notable genre titles in the '80s. Neil Jordan's lyrical
and creepy *The Company of Wolves* and Bernard Rose's intriguing *Paperhouse* both
explored the darker side of children's fantasies, while Ken Russell did Mary Shelley in
the ponderous *Gothic* and Bram Stoker in the outrageously entertaining *Lair of the
White Worm*. Finally, horror author Clive Barker directed the superior *Hellraiser*; it was
followed by Tony Randel's intense sequel, *Hellbound: Hellraiser II*. Unfortunately,
Barker's most recent film, the flawed but fascinating *Nightbreed*, was dumped by its
American distributor.

Meanwhile, in the States, a fresh new crop of filmmakers were making their mark
with graphic, uncompromising features. A college-age director named Sam Raimi delivered *The Evil Dead*, which featured the scariest use of ultraviolence and some of the
most dazzling camerawork the genre had ever seen. Joel Coen, an editor on *Evil Dead*,
teamed with his brother Ethan to make *Blood Simple*, a popular cross between the film
noir and splatter genres. Frank Henenlotter turned out *Basket Case*, the weirdest story
of brotherly love imaginable, and followed it up with the boy-and-his-parasite tale,
Brain Damage. Following a string of successful, visceral stage plays, Stuart Gordon
turned the mad scientist genre on its, uh, head with *Re-Animator*. *Alien* scripter Dan
O'Bannon became a director with *The Return of the Living Dead*, which pumped
comic blood into the zombie subgenre. And from down in New Zealand came *Bad*

Taste, Peter Jackson's splattery comedy shocker about aliens whose favorite fast food is human flesh.

It's ironic that so many of these graphic successes (along with Raimi's *Evil Dead II*) utilized humorous elements, as the horror comedy was one of the most reviled trends of the '80s. The aforementioned and a couple of mainstream hits (Ivan Reitman's *Ghostbusters* and Tim Burton's *Beetlejuice*) notwithstanding, the subgenre gave us a series of turkeys like *Transylvania 6-5000*, *Teen Wolf* and *Teen Wolf Too*, *Saturday the 14th*, *Haunted Honeymoon*, *Student Bodies* and *National Lampoon's Class Reunion*; *House* and *C.H.U.D.*, which effectively blended scares and laughs, were both followed by dumb, jokey sequels.

Getting back to the big-budget side of things, the major studios started pumping more money than ever before into genre films, with mixed results: Steven Spielberg produced *Poltergeist*, a dazzling ghost story directed (some say only nominally) by Tobe Hooper; Joe Dante's *Gremlins*, a viciously satirical monster movie whose violence helped inspire the creation of the PG-13 rating; and *Arachnophobia*, Frank Marshall's effective update of the old "attack of the killer spiders" story. Other big-name directors to tackle the genre, with varying degrees of success, included John Irvin (*Ghost Story*), Michael Wadleigh (*Wolfen*), Paul Schrader (*Cat People*), Jack Clayton (*Something Wicked This Way Comes*), Michael Mann (*The Keep*), Franc Roddam (*The Bride*), Alan Parker (*Angel Heart*), John Schlesinger (*The Believers*) and George Cosmatos (*Leviathan*). Oliver Stone and Tony Scott made their major-studio debuts with *The Hand* and *The Hunger* respectively, before moving to bigger projects.

The studios also gave the independent superstars of the '70s their shot at bigtime, mainstream moviemaking. But first, almost every one of them worked for Avco Embassy, which was without a doubt the most valuable independent studio of the early '80s. With a talent for keeping production costs low and giving their product solid promotion, Avco provided a stepping stone to the big leagues for John Carpenter (*The Fog* and *Escape from New York*), Joe Dante (*The Howling*), David Cronenberg (*Scanners*), Wes Craven (*Swamp Thing*), Don Coscarelli (*Phantasm*) and others.

Once he moved on, Carpenter made *The Thing*, the film version of Stephen King's *Christine*, the critical hit *Starman* and the genre-blender *Big Trouble in Little China*. Bummed by his studio experiences on *Big Trouble*, Carpenter retreated to the lower-budgeted, uneven but interesting *Prince of Darkness* and *They Live*. Dante followed up *Gremlins* with the science-fiction comedies *Explorers* and *Innerspace*, lost his footing with *The 'Burbs* and found it again with the hilarious *Gremlins 2: The New Batch*. Craven's checkered career veered from the high of *A Nightmare on Elm Street* to the low of *Deadly Friend*, with *The Serpent and the Rainbow* and *Shocker* landing somewhere in between. Coscarelli had a flop with the sword-and-sorcery tale *The Beastmaster*, then disappeared for a while before reappearing with *Phantasm II*.

A couple of other horror veterans rose through the ranks without Avco's assistance. Tobe Hooper never lived up to his *Chainsaw Massacre* promise; his string of '80s films (from *The Funhouse* to *Spontaneous Combustion*) ranged from mediocre to embarrassing. Tom Holland, who wrote *The Beast Within* and *Psycho II* among others, directed the crowd-pleasing *Fright Night* and *Child's Play*. Horror's most eccentric and erratic talent, Larry Cohen, made a string of quirky B-flicks ranging from the inspired monster pic *Q* through a pair of interesting sequels (*It's Alive III* and *Return to Salem's Lot*), ending with the disastrous *Wicked Stepmother*.

Two of the most exciting directors to make major films in the '80s, however, were Cronenberg and George Romero. Before rounding off his zombie trilogy with the intense *Day of the Dead*, Romero directed *Creepshow*, a stylish homage to EC horror comics that enjoyed a successful national release. He was not so lucky with his first studio production, *Monkey Shines*; a chilling, engrossing story of good, evil and the animal within us all, it was mishandled by its distributor and sank without a trace. Cronenberg had better luck; after his absorbing, *very* strange *Videodrome* flopped, he had a modest hit with the excellent King-inspired *The Dead Zone*. Then came *The Fly*, a gruesome but challenging remake that was a hit with critics and audiences. Cronenberg won more raves with *Dead Ringers*, though the story of twin gynecologists and their strange psychic bond turned off the mainstream audience.

Finally, there was James Cameron, the last of the Corman graduates to really hit it big. After working as a designer and FX man on *Galaxy of Terror* and others, he segued into directing with the forgettable *Piranha II: The Spawning*, but followed it up only a year later with *The Terminator*. Then came his crowning achievement: *Aliens*, which outdid Ridley Scott's *Alien* in both thrills and box office.

Two minitrends of the '80s are worth noting. One was the rush to adapt anything written by Stephen King to the screen; in addition to the aforementioned, there was Mark Lester's *Firestarter*, Fritz Kiersch's *Children of the Corn*, Daniel Attias' *Silver Bullet* and King's own directorial debut, *Maximum Overdrive*. Dwindling box office kept King off the screen for a while, but in 1989, Mary Lambert's *Pet Sematary* was a smash, and was followed by Ralph Singleton's *Graveyard Shift* and Rob Reiner's excellent *Misery*. There was also the (brief) return of 3-D, spearheaded by Charles Band's low-budget *Parasite*, emboldened by the hit *Friday the 13th Part III* and quickly killed by *Jaws 3-D* and Band's *Metalstorm*.

A much more important and lasting technological development was the video invasion, which had more influence on the horror genre than any trend in recent memory. At first, it seemed that all the new cassette market offered was advantages; it was a new way to see your favorite films, unreleased titles could find their way into the light and box-office flops had a new shot at success. Video also provided a new forum for independent filmmakers to show off their talent without the high costs attendant to feature film production.

Unfortunately, for every amateur auteur who turned a low budget to his advan-

YESTERDAY'S B-MOVIE BECAME TODAY'S $17-MILLION SPECTACULAR, DELIVERING A *Blob* TRULY WORTH BEWARING.

© TriStar

tage, like campmeister Mark (*Curse of the Queerwolf*) Pirro, there were a dozen hacks turning out backyard disasters like *Lunchmeat, Cannibal Campout, Truth or Dare, 555* and others. In addition, the emphasis on name recognition in the video market-place led to a flock of unnecessary sequels. Only the brand-name mentality of the cassette industry could inspire five *Howling* retreads, four *Silent Night, Deadly Night* sequels, two more *Sleepaway Camp*s, etc., etc.

Video really took its toll on the midrange independent distributors. As viewers found that they could wait and see the same films for a $2 rental instead of an increasingly expensive movie ticket, many independent companies overextended themselves with higher-budgeted films and nationwide saturation releases. Despite Michael Douglas' pronouncements in *Wall Street*, greed was not good for Cannon, Atlantic, Vestron, New World and, most sadly, Avco Embassy, which was sold to Norman Lear and collapsed shortly thereafter. Promising talent in the low-budget horror field was still recognized by the majors, but with a couple of exceptions, John (*Nomads*) McTiernan, Kathryn (*Near Dark*) Bigelow, Renny (*Prison*) Harlin, Joseph (*The Stepfather*) Ruben, Rowdy (*Jack's Back*) Herrington and, most recently, John McNaughton, all went directly to big-studio action thrillers without passing Go.

Things briefly looked bright for independent horror in 1984, when Charles Band formed Empire Pictures for the expressed purpose of providing a new outlet for genre product. But overambition and a string of bad movies put a damper on Band's bid to become the next Roger Corman, though he reappeared shortly after Empire's fall with the direct-to-video Full Moon company. Corman himself continued to turn out exploitation product through his new Concorde Pictures, but sadly, their overall quality couldn't live up to the glory days of the '70s.

Oh, by the way, you've probably noticed that there's been no mention of a certain razor-fingered villain who became the biggest terror icon of the decade. But look at it this way: Anyone who has been following the modern horror genre undoubtedly knows more about him than could be summed up here in a few paragraphs.

TOP 13 HORROR FILMS OF THE '80s

The Howling (1981)
Poltergeist (1981)
The Thing (1982)
The Evil Dead (1983)
A Nightmare on Elm Street (1984)
Re-Animator (1985)
Aliens (1986)
The Fly (1986)
Hellraiser (1987)
The Stepfather (1987)
The Blob (1988)
Monkey Shines (1988)
Henry: Portrait of a Serial Killer (1989)

© Paramount

AS ONE OF *Friday the 13th* **ENTRIES' MANY GIMMICKS, JASON TOOK MANHATTAN . . . BUT THE AUDIENCE TOOK A NAP.**

H. P. LOVECRAFT: THE UNADAPTABLE?

BY WILL MURRAY

Wouldn't it be great if we could dig up H.P. Lovecraft and give him a good shot of Herbert West's day-glo elixir? Think of the possibilities. We could get him to write more stories. Insist he tell us how to pronounce "Cthulhu." And then, after we'd sucked him dry of every drop of eldritch lore, treat him to a marathon Lovecraft film festival just to see the look on his face when he discovers how a generation of filmmakers have adapted his work.

In the absence of a way to reanimate HPL, we'll have to settle for what he left us. And we can only guess what he might have made of the flood of film adaptations of his works that have spewed forth over the last few years. Certainly he'd be shocked by their sheer number, if not numbed by the incredible liberties taken.

After all, this is the man who walked out in the middle of Tod Browning's *Dracula* back in 1931, and a year later forced himself to sit through the classic James Whale *Frankenstein*, only to pronounce it disappointing. Lovecraft's idea of a great movie was *Winterset* or *Berkeley Square*, hard as that may be for us, his late 20th-century fans, to imagine.

During his lifetime, Lovecraft had only one known brush with the specter of adaptation. His *Weird Tales* editor, Farnsworth Wright, expressed interest in buying from Lovecraft the radio adaptation rights to his "Dreams in the Witch-House" when he first bought the story in 1933. Despite needing the money, Lovecraft turned down the offer cold.

"It is not likely," the author told Wright, "that *any* really finely wrought weird story—where so much depends upon mood, and on nuances of description—could be changed to a drama without irreparable cheapening and the loss of all that gave it power."

He later confided to a correspondent, "I shall never permit anything bearing my signature to be banalized and vulgarized into the kind of flat infantile twaddle which passes for 'horror tales' amongst radio and cinema audiences!"

Re-Animator **ESTABLISHED A HIGH-WATER MARK FOR CINEMATIC LOVECRAFT ADAPTATIONS.**

Of course, H.P. Lovecraft died in 1937, at age 46. If he *were* alive today, he would be 103—and probably a hell of a lot crankier than he was in his prime.

The awful truth is the Old Gentleman would never have let his stories reach the screen in the first place. And if any *had* slipped through the copyright cracks, he might have found little to praise. Certainly he would have had no kind words for the trio of American International Pictures productions which were the first big-screen treatments of his classic stories.

Lovecraft would have been flabbergasted had he lived to see AIP's 1963 movie *The Haunted Palace.* Based upon his only novel, *The Case of Charles Dexter Ward*, it was released as part of AIP's Edgar Allan Poe series. The title is taken from a Poe poem which star Vincent Price recites just before the action begins.

Whether Lovecraft would have been flattered by being linked with Poe long enough to sit through *The Haunted Palace* makes for fascinating speculation. What he would have found bears only a passing resemblance to his original tale of Charles Dexter Ward, doomed to be possessed by his evil warlock ancestor, Joseph Curwen. The locale is shifted from Lovecraft's beloved home town of Providence to the mythical Arkham, Massachusetts—on the theory, no doubt, that Arkham is more Lovecraftian. All the great stuff about calling up the dead through their "essential salts" is reduced to drive-in movie black magic. Ho hum.

THE AUTHOR'S FORMLESS TERRORS DEFY EASY VISUALIZATION, BUT TODD MASTERS' FX FOR *The Resurrected* GAVE IT A GOOD TRY.

OK, so they kept the character names and threw out virtually everything else. At least they cast Vincent Price as Curwen/Ward and hired *Twilight Zone*'s Charles Beaumont to script the film—although rumor has it that Beaumont wasn't much of a Lovecraft fan. Any movie that stars Vincent Price is worth watching on its own merits, and *The Haunted Palace* is no exception.

AIP's next Lovecraft outing was also set in Arkham—Arkham, England, that is. *Die, Monster, Die!* (1965) was titled *Monster of Terror* in Great Britain, where it was filmed. Based upon one of Lovecraft's greatest stories, "The Colour Out of Space," *Die, Monster, Die!* featured Nick Adams, Suzan Farmer and a failing Boris Karloff trapped in a slow mix of mad-scientist madness that had more in common with "The Fall of the House of Usher" than it had with Lovecraft. The author's blight-causing meteorite, which houses a gaseous creature of no known color may not be easily filmable, but here it's reduced to a mere radioactive rock that triggers low-budget mutations.

Roger Corman produced the final AIP effort, *The Dunwich Horror* (1970), directed by Daniel (*Die, Monster, Die!*) Haller. It's closer to its roots than the previous films, and more experimental. "The Dunwich Horror" is possibly the most adaptable of all Lovecraft stories because it has a protagonist and a good-wins-over-evil ending. In fact, the radio show *Suspense* did an excellent Orson Wellesian adaptation of it back in 1945.

Corman does not. Despite some interesting casting—Dean Stockwell as the strange Wilbur Whateley, Ed Begley as old Wizard Whateley and Sandra Dee as the obligatory pretty young thing Lovecraft scrupulously kept out of his stories—the action simply flounders around until popping like a burst soap bubble when the most malign entity in Lovecraft's repertoire, Yog-Sothoth, finally appears. He looks suspiciously like a giant sea anemone. Corman also changed the ending, so that the bad guys win! Only he could have made the story more Lovecraftian than Lovecraft had written it.

After *Dunwich*, Lovecraftian film adaptations ceased. The 1967 Warner Bros. Gothic, *The Shuttered Room*, was advertised as written by "H.P. Lovecraft and August Derleth." Derleth was Lovecraft's posthumous publisher, the founder of Arkham House, who liked to turn old Lovecraft ideas into new stories and call them collaborations. Lovecraft had as much to do with Derleth's story as you or I—and I don't know about you, but I didn't add a word.

One of Boris Karloff's final films, *The Crimson Cult* (1970), is sometimes said to be based on Lovecraft because it is set in Arkham. Despite suspicious resemblance to "The Dreams in the Witch-House," it is not an adaptation, nor is it worth discussing.

There were two Lovecraft adaptations on Rod Serling's classic *Night Gallery* TV series: a good version of a lame story ("Cool Air") and a bad version of a good story ("Pickman's Model"). The problem with "Pickman's Model" is that they showed the monster: Lovecraft's creatures are generally too horrific to show on film. And when they are presented as stuntmen in latex suits, they look silly.

Ironically, while Lovecraft's work only began to achieve widespread paperback exposure in the early 1970s, Lovecraft films simply didn't get made for most of the '70s and '80s. That all changed when Charles Band's Empire Pictures brought out *Re-Animator* in 1985.

It's not hard to imagine Lovecraft's reaction to this film: He would have run screaming from the theater in horror. First, it was based on a serial he penned in 1921 for *Home Brew*, a humor magazine on the same level as *Mad*. Lovecraft hated writing "Grewsome Tales," as "Herbert West—Reanimator" was originally titled, even though it was obviously a deadpan satire of *Frankenstein*, and later struck it from his list of acknowledged stories. Secondly, the extremely graphic sex and violence would have repelled the Old Gent worse than a calamari calzone. He detested sex, violence and seafood. Possibly in that order.

If Lovecraft had lasted till 1985, he would have sued the pants off director Stuart Gordon before letting *Re-Animator* get into the theaters. But he would have lost, because "Herbert West—Reanimator" was by then in the public domain, not to mention a treasure. The strange truth is that *Re-Animator* remains the most faithful to the spirit of the original of all Lovecraftian films to date. Many of the best scenes—such as Dr. Hill's use of a wax head to get past the morgue guard—are taken directly from the story, although reshuffled like so many Tarot cards. The original, by the way, was not a short story, but a collection of episodic tales featuring Herbert West, whom Lovecraft dubbed "that languid Elagabalus of the tombs," and sometimes denigrated as "that cursed little towhead fiend."

Everyone knows what happened after *Re-Animator* took audiences and critics by storm: Anyone who could lay hands on a Lovecraft story tried to bring it to the screen. Empire announced *The Lurking Fear*, predictably Lovecraft's only other *Home Brew* story. They also filmed "The Evil Clergyman" as one of three segments for the planned anthology film *Pulse Pounders*. Then they went belly-up—but not before they released *From Beyond*.

Another Stuart Gordon project, *From Beyond* (1986) was an FX-heavy extravaganza that was almost a literal adaptation of the Lovecraft story of the same name. The problem was the original story was only 10 pages long, and Gordon dispensed with the entire thing before the opening credits started to roll. The footage after the credits was actually a kind of sequel to the precredit sequence.

The main story had the disconcerting feel of a *Re-Animator* reunion on downers, with Jeffrey Combs playing the too-solemn Dr. Crawford Tillinghast and Barbara Crampton as a too-prim love interest, Dr. Katherine McMichaels. Everyone involved seemed to be taking all the psychosexual weirdness too seriously to pull it off. After the hilarity of *Re-Animator*, some audiences found *From Beyond* turgid and disappointing. But that didn't stop other filmmakers from bringing out new Lovecraft films.

Trans World's *The Curse* (1987) was another adaptation of "The Colour Out of Space." This time the setting was transplanted from Arkham to Tennessee's Tellico Plains, and Lovecraft's evocative masterpiece became nothing more than a vehicle for redneck angst run amuck. You couldn't even call it a remake of *Die, Monster, Die!*; star Wil Wheaton played a character not found in either the AIP film or the original story. The best part of *The Curse* was Claude Akins' over-the-top-and-through-the-woods acting—if you like that sort of thing. Lovecraft would have puked tentacles; "Colour" was his favorite story. The same year also witnessed the direct-to-video release *Forever Evil*, which adapted its monster-god's name (Yog Kathoth) and little else from the author's writings.

The Unnamable (1988) was another very short Lovecraft tale that was put on the rack and stretched by a fiendish scriptwriter into a too-long direct-to-video movie. It featured the usual Lovecraftian trappings: Miskatonic University students (Randolph Carter and Charles Dexter Ward, both lifted from completely different Lovecraft stories!) stumbling across the inevitable copy of the *Necronomicon*, blundering into a haunted house and gibbering in horror at What They Find. The only thing to keep one awake through this flick was a clever creature that, unfortunately, didn't have much to do with the original story, which was about a horror so beyond the pale it could neither be described nor named. Lovecraft would have pointed out the sad fact that the monster was merely a harpy out of Greek mythology.

TOP RIGHT
DR. PRETORIOUS
EMERGES *From
Beyond* IN ALL HIS
HORRIFIC
SPLENDOR.

The most notable recent Lovecraftian entry was the long-awaited *Bride of Re-Animator* (1991), fresh from a two-year stint on the distributor's shelf. Just like the head of Dr. Hill, whose discovery triggers a new investigation into the now-classic Miskatonic Massacre.

Once again, snippets of the original story are woven into a reasonably organic whole. The opening scene, depicting West and Dan Cain having fun with the casualties in a Peruvian civil war, comes from the printed installment where they performed much the same blasphemies upon World War I wounded. And the climax, featuring a legion of the reanimated dead wreaking vengeance upon West, is just Lovecraft's original ending cranked up a few decibels. But where *Re-Animator* was fresh, it was also hard to top, and *Bride* does not quite succeed. It needed Stuart Gordon. Or maybe Brian Yuzna, looking for an R rating—or any rating at all—simply tamed the twitchy West and company too much to pull off a miracle twice in a row.

Since it owes as much to Mary Shelley as H.P. Lovecraft—which Yuzna duly acknowledges in the closing credits—*Bride of Re-Animator* is a kind of *Haunted Palace* in reverse. This time, it's Lovecraft's name being used to sell a partial adaptation of another writer's concept. Somehow, one doubts Lovecraft would have been amused.

Still, *Bride of Re-Animator* is the second most faithful Lovecraft adaptation to date. But it isn't the quintessential Lovecraft we're seeing, but Lovecraft the parodist.

Still more Lovecraft Films hit the small screen in recent years. Unsurprisingly, Juan Piquer Simon's Spanish direct-to-video schlocker *Cthulhu Mansion* had little to do with "The Call of Cthulhu." HBO's cable movie, *Cast a Deadly Spell*, was a period detective story decorated with HPL-inspired beasts. It may work, but it won't be true Lovecraft. There were no private eyes in his world.

TOP LEFT
The Bride of Re-Animator
**WORE RED, THANKS
TO THE WORK OF
KNB EFX.**

TOP RIGHT
The Unnamable Returns
**COMBINED NOT ONE
BUT TWO HPL
STORIES, THE
SECOND BEING "THE
STATEMENT OF
RANDOLPH CARTER."**

Dan O'Bannon's *The Resurrected*, another adaptation of *The Case of Charles Dexter Ward*, was well-received by fans when it hit video in 1992, even though the book is not Lovecraft's most representative work. In fact, while he wrote a complete draft, the author never revised it for publication or submitted it anywhere in his lifetime. This may be a case where Lovecraft would have sued to prevent his *own story* from reaching print, never mind going before the cameras. He considered it unfinished.

Will we ever see the real H.P. Lovecraft up there on the silver screen? Can "The Call of Cthulhu" be filmed? Will *At the Mountains of Madness* or the classic "Shadow Out of Time" be done with the eerie power of the very Lovecraftian *Alien*? Will *The Shadow Over Innsmouth* ever go before the cameras?

The great Lovecraft adaptations have yet to be made. That more films *will* be made is certain; whether they will live up to their source material remains to be seen. H.P. Lovecraft most often wrote of mood and emotion. He wove his magic not by shoving the reader's face into a squirming mass of tentacles, but by letting us glimpse, in the lightning flash of an instant, the tip of the unknown questing into our terrestrial real world, and touching us with the mixture of dread awe and delicious anticipation that compelled him to weave his nebulous horrors.

As Lovecraft once explained his literary aims, "My reason for writing stories is to give myself the satisfaction of visualizing more clearly and detailedly and stably the vague, elusive, fragmentary impressions of wonder, beauty, and adventurous expectancy which are conveyed to me by certain sights (scenic, architectural, atmospheric, etc.), ideas, occurrences, and images encountered in art and literature. I choose weird stories because they suit my inclination best—one of my strongest and most persistent wishes being to achieve, momentarily, the illusion of some strange suspension or violation of the galling limitations of time, space and natural law which forever imprison us and frustrate our curiosity about the infinite cosmic spaces beyond the tradition of our sight and analysis."

In other words, Lovecraft considered his work less about monsters and horror than about mood and metaphysics. He was a cosmic visionary. The director who brings the real Lovecraft to the screen will have to be a towering visionary in the same mold. Perhaps he's reading these words even now.

WIL WHEATON RAN AFOUL OF *The Curse* IN ONE OF THE SCHLOCKIER LOVECRAFT PIX.

ORIGINS OF THE LIVING DEAD

BY ANTHONY TIMPONE

DON'T HOLD YOUR BREATH FOR ROMERO TO RETURN TO THE LAND OF THE LIVING DEAD ANYTIME SOON.

By now, the making of the original Night of the Living Dead *is the stuff of legend. It's the story of how a group of independent Pittsburgh commercial producers decided to pool together a meager $114,000 and make a "monster movie" in their own backyard. Working in intensive spurts between paying assignments, writer/director George Romero, co-writer/producer John Russo, producer/actors Karl Hardman ("Harry Cooper") and Russ Streiner ("Johnny") and others broke their butts and bank accounts to deliver a genre breakthrough.*

Another tale of legend (and sad truth) is an unscrupulous distributor's pocketing of most of Romero and company's profits when the film opened in 1968 to considerable success on the drive-in and midnight movie circuits. The raking that the investors took led to most of the same group reteaming to remake NOTLD in 1990. Directed by makeup FX artist Tom Savini and scripted by Romero, the new version flopped at the box office. Interviewed on the set of NOTLD 1990, Romero discussed the creation of his 1968 black-and-white classic.

FANGORIA: Describe a typical day on the set of the original *Night of the Living Dead.*

GEORGE A. ROMERO: Things were pretty frantic then because we were doing beer commercials on the side—actually, we were doing beer commercials principally and *Night of the Living Dead* on the side! So it was pretty nuts. We were living in the farmhouse, so we'd get up and take a bath in the creek and start to shoot, and we just shot day and night, day and night. It was definitely a family environment.

FANG: What made the first film so successful?

ROMERO: We got incredibly lucky. We had a lot of good fortune with that movie. First of all, it was black and white; it was angry; it reflected our attitudes and the attitudes of the times. We finished it before we ever had a distributor and literally threw a finished print in the trunk of a car, and Russ Streiner and I drove to New York with it on the night that Martin Luther King was shot. That just puts it in a framework in terms of what the times were like. And the fact that it had a black man in a lead role that didn't have to be played by a black man, and that it had some sociopolitical criticism or satire in it, made some people elevate the film and make it into a work of art. Every film to me is a work of art; it is the work of artists. But *NOTLD* was maybe given too much credit for something that wasn't its primary purpose. Those attitudes and subtexts crept into it because that was the way we were thinking at the time, and it's because of those influences having crept into the film that it was made into something more important than a midnight movie.

At the same time, there was a whole group of people in this country who were saying that we needed a rating system, and *Night of the Living Dead* was one of those movies that the people pointed to and said, "Look, see? That's why we need a ratings board! Look what these guys are doing! They're corrupting us, and corrupting our children. . ."

So those two things came together and lifted the film out of the pack. And in addition, there are sequences in the film that really work and are scary. There are these creatures out there. . . the threat is very mundane; on the one hand, they're the neighbors, but in some cases the neighbors are the most frightening people you ever face.

FANG: What scenes jolted audiences the most in 1968?

ROMERO: The cannibalism scenes were probably the ones that people

IN THE ROMERO-PRODUCED *Night* REMAKE, BARBARA WAS BETTER ABLE TO TAKE CARE OF HERSELF.

most pointed to. We didn't cut away when that stuff happened. In other parts of the film, it's very traditional; you don't see the trowel enter flesh. But in the cannibalism sequences we didn't cut away, and that was the one area where it just went another couple of inches beyond what people had seen before. That's why people thought it should have had an X rating. At that time there was no such thing as an X.

FANG: What is the movie's real theme?

ROMERO: The lack of communication. Human communication has always been the movie's theme. It's a theme that I've often worked with. These people can't even talk to each other long enough in an organized way to figure out how to escape. They could actually escape very easily, but because of their own problems and inability to communicate, they don't succeed.

FANG: Was that and other themes intentional when you first started filming?

ROMERO: That theme was certainly purposeful in the script. We talked about it a lot: that, thematically, is what's happening. It's very hard when you're working on something and building it, you don't know which way it's going to go. It's like when you're sculpting and you don't know: ''Gee, if I do this, what's gonna happen? Let me try it. And if that works, I'll keep that, and I'll add this and add that.'' So it stays pliable until you finally see it and are gluing it together, and then you can put those finishing touches on it.

FANG: What made you select a horror movie as your first effort?

ROMERO: We had actually tried to do several other features prior to this! [*Laughs*] We could never get financing, we could never get enough people enthused to actually kick in their own money, which is the way *Night of the Living Dead* started—10 of us kicked in our own money and started the company, and then went around to 20 other friends and relatives and got more money from them! The earlier features that we tried to do just never got off the ground. We could never get the same kind of enthusiasm. So we decided to do something that had a more commercial identification, a horror movie, which was fine with me because I've always loved the genre. I'm happy to be working in it.

FANG: Did any filmmakers influence your early work?

ROMERO: It's a very parasitic medium, and you never get to sketch, so you're always either consciously or unconsciously imitating or stealing from other people. I know that several people have written about me, and they say my stuff is a lot like Hitchcock, and that's probably not true. In the case of *Night of the Living Dead*, it probably borrows or steals more directly from Orson Welles than it does from anyone else. Just the lighting style and the radical angles call up a little bit of *Macbeth* or *Citizen Kane*. Not that it achieves it as well, but if I had anything in mind at the time, it was that.

FANG: Did you expect *NOTLD* to change the face of modern horror and shock the world?

ROMERO: No, we did not expect that *at all!* We thought we were making a little movie, and if we were lucky it would go out and show in the drive-ins, and we would turn a little profit and take it and reinvest it and make another little movie. That's really as far ahead as we thought.

FANG: Why has the film stood the test of time?

ROMERO: That's part of that other question; it's because it became such a curiosity, and because it became so identified with social satire, and was invited into the Museum of Modern Art. That gave it a permanence. In addition to that, and this was another aspect of luck, it became one of those midnight movies, one of those movies that people

THE LIVING DEAD
ROSE AGAIN IN
FANTACO'S *NOTLD*
COMIC ADAPTATION.

© Laurel

went to goof on and recite the dialogue to, and sit and watch over and over.

FANG: When did you and your Latent Image partners first realize that you had a hit on your hands?

ROMERO: *Night* had a very slow growth; it took a very long time for the film to be successful on the level that it's been successful. It was making money in moderate amounts almost immediately out in drive-ins, which is what we were hoping that it would do. We were celebrating more for the fact that we completed the job than for its success. All of us involved in the film's making were people who loved movies and wanted desperately to *make* movies. I always thought making movies was something done by elves in Hollywoodland or something, and all of a sudden we made this movie. And so there was this big moment when we had the opening premiere and we were actually showing a movie we made in one of the downtown theaters here. That was a very big moment for me; it was the very first time I'd seen something I did, and all of us felt the same way, seeing it on a big screen. And during that first week the

film played, we all went out with Karl Hardman, who had this big old sedan, got some popcorn and watched it at a drive-in! And that was a big moment too, because we could actually go out and see one of our movies at a drive-in, man! We were in the big time.

FANG: In your wildest dreams, did you ever imagine you'd be shooting a remake 22 years later?

ROMERO: Not then, no; I would never have thought that. I don't know if it's a dubious distinction, but I'm one of three living directors who's been colorized *and* remade. As I said, none of us thought it would be this kind of success.

FANG: If the investors hadn't gotten burned on the first film, would you still have remade *NOTLD*?

ROMERO: I don't know. Because we got so ripped off on the original release, I'm really sympathetic to the idea of the original investors finally—hopefully—making some money. And if the remake can help that, and if the colorization can help that, great.

**TOP LEFT
SADLY, THE REMAKE OF *NOTLD* WAS NOT THE FINANCIAL HIT ITS BACKERS HOPED FOR.**

**TOP RIGHT
ROMERO FOLLOWED HIS ZOMBIE CLASSIC WITH *Dawn of the Dead*, THE SECOND FILM OF THE TRILOGY.**

BY W.C. STROBY

STEPHEN KING'S CINEMA CATS AND DOGS

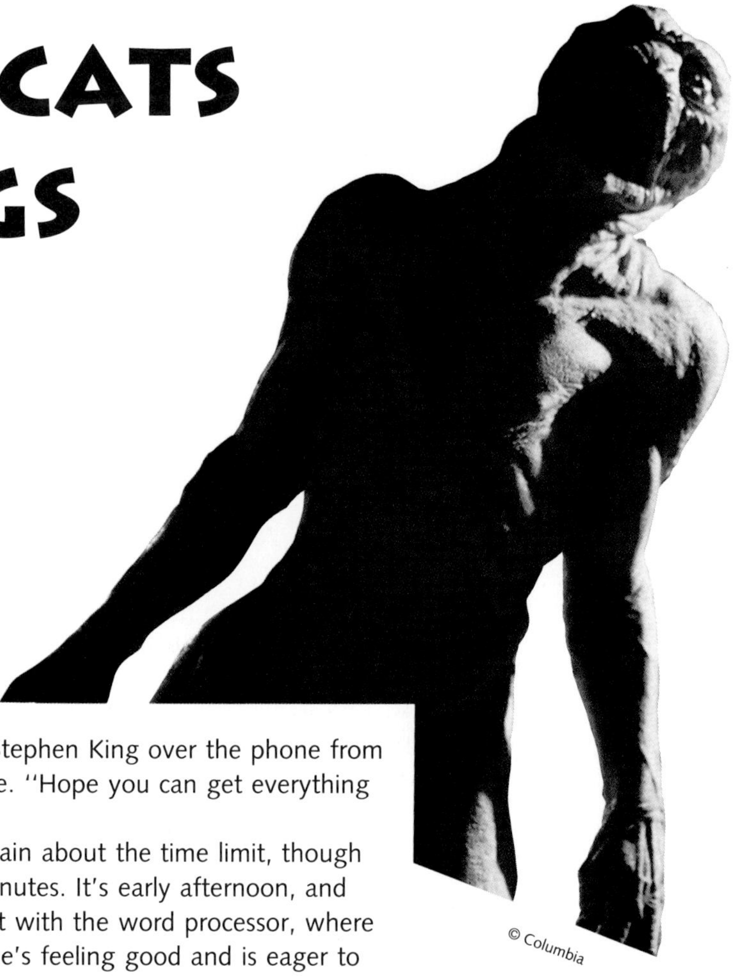

© Columbia

SOMEONE MUST HAVE TOLD THIS SLEEPWALKER THAT THE MPAA FORCED CUTS OF HIS FIRST FILM.

H i, how you doing?" says Stephen King over the phone from his office in Bangor, Maine. "Hope you can get everything you need in a half hour."

It's difficult to complain about the time limit, though it's hard to imagine covering his output in just 30 minutes. It's early afternoon, and King is fresh from his daily four-and-a-half-hour bout with the word processor, where he is finishing up the final draft of his latest novel. He's feeling good and is eager to talk, and the 30 minutes quickly stretch to 45. Despite repeated insistences that he has to go, he's always willing to field one final question—and then the one after that.

The last few years have shaped up to be big ones for King and, unsurprisingly enough, he's excited about that fact. Winter 1992 saw the publication of his novel *The Waste Lands*, the third installment in a cycle of stories collectively known as *The Dark Tower*. The series, which began with the publication of *The Gunslinger* in 1982, chronicles the odyssey of an enigmatic gunfighter named Roland and his quest for the mysterious Dark Tower. (The fourth book, *Wizard and Glass*, is due out in 1994, coming after King's 26th novel, *Gerald's Game*, its follow-up, *Dolores Claiborne*, and the short-story collection *Nightmares and Dreamscapes*.)

In addition to Mick Garris' *Sleepwalkers*, King's first filmed original screenplay, a host of film projects bearing King's name unspooled at movie theaters throughout 1992 and '93. New Line's *The Lawnmower Man*, starring Pierce Brosnan and Jeff Fahey, expands a brief story from King's *Night Shift* collection into a hi-tech science-fiction thriller rooted in cybernetics and virtual reality (the same producers are also planning a film based on "The Mangler," another *Night Shift* entry). Meanwhile,

George Romero's take on *The Dark Half*, starring Timothy Hutton as both troubled author Thad Beaumont and his murderous alter ego George Stark, opened in April 1993 after nearly two years in limbo, along with numerous other films produced by financially-troubled Orion Pictures.

King is less than enthusiastic about two theatrical sequels released during this period: Miramax/Dimension's *Children of the Corn II* and Paramount's *Pet Sematary II*. Though he is associated with the films in name only—and their timing makes him less than happy—there's no mistaking that rumbling sound in the distance. The Stephen King juggernaut is up and rolling again, augmenting the 140 million copies of his books in print, the more than two dozen films made from his works and the nearly 30 books already written about him.

FANGORIA: How do you feel about the way *Sleepwalkers* came out? What percentage of your original vision ended up in the film?

STEPHEN KING: *Sleepwalkers* came out real well. On a grading scale—if an A is 92 to 100 and a B is 84 to 91—I'd probably give it a B-plus. In terms of how much of my original vision is on the screen, the problems with that are always in the same place, and people who read FANGORIA know all about this. The movie was submitted to the censors—[MPAA president] Jack Valenti calls them the ratings board, but what they are are censors—and the picture came back NC-17, which meant it had to be resubmitted [to get an R]. So the fact remains that how much of my vision remains in the film is not in the hands of myself or my director, but in the hands of a bunch of people whom I'll never see and who probably are not fans of my stuff.

FANG: What was the genesis of the story? Was it an idea you had around for a while?

KING: No, it was based on something that my older son, Joe, was going through. He was about 17 at the time—around the age of Charles Brady, who is the villain of *Sleepwalkers*—and he had this real crisis where he wanted to date this cute girl named Karen, who worked at the local Hoyts Cinema. And he was experiencing all the typical things teenage boys go through when they want to ask out some girl who's really neat.

So we listened to a lot of agoniz-

ing at my house about Joe's crush on this popcorn girl, and one night when we were at the movies, he was talking to her and I saw why he was attracted to her. She was just this beautiful, vital girl who played a lot of sports and had this kind of healthy, wholesome glow about her. And it occurred to me then that girls always get asked for dates, and that sometimes the people who ask them are potentially dangerous; but if they're charming, there's no way of differentiating the people who are OK from the people who are dangerous. And that made me think of a guy wanting to ask the popcorn girl out for all the wrong reasons, and the story just sort of followed that burst of inspiration. So, in a sense, my son was the prototype for the bad guy this time.

FANG: But the idea came to you as a screenplay rather than a novel?

KING: It was never an idea for a novel, and the reason why was because it was set in a movie theater to begin with. The other thing was that it didn't come to me in a series of ideas, the way a lot of the books do, but a series of images.

The business about approaching the popcorn girl came to me, and after that I started to see the scene where the main character's mother would come to the house of the girl's parents, carrying this vase of flowers, and shatter the vase across the face of either the mother or the father. I had no idea why at that point, but the image was extremely violent and extremely powerful for me. That was what energized me to find the

And I would argue with these people at the studios and say, "Well, does cancer make rational sense in the end? Do birth defects make rational sense in the end?" What I wanted to talk about in the screenplay were the things that come out of nowhere and drive you nuts, and there's no real answer to them.

But they just gave me these sort of blank stares. They've got these odd, maddening, literal minds in Hollywood. There has to be a reason for everything.

NO DOUBT THE POPCORN GIRL AT KING'S HOMETOWN THEATER WILL BE ROOTING FOR *Sleepwalkers'* **MADCHEN AMICK.**

BELOW IN THE *Cat's Eye* **TRADITION, FELINES ARE THE HEROES OF KING'S LATEST SCREEN SHOCKER.**

link that held those two scenes together —the guy meeting the popcorn girl and then the mother of the guy hurting the parents with the vase. And both of those scenes made it into the movie.

FANG: Have you written any other original screenplays?

KING: I wrote a screenplay about 12 years ago called *The Shotgunners* that Sam Peckinpah was interested in. We had meetings with Peckinpah and he liked it. He was in New York looking for projects, and we got together at the UN Plaza Hotel and talked about it for quite a while.

Peckinpah was real bright and real clear about some of the things that he thought could be done with the script. These were things that actually would have helped it; they weren't studio bull-shit, because he wasn't with a studio at that time. But when we met, he was very frail and obviously not well. He died of a heart attack shortly thereafter, so nothing ever happened with the screenplay.

The thing about *The Shotgunners* is that nobody in Hollywood wanted to have anything to do with it, because it didn't make rational sense at the end.

But if there's a car chase and shots fired and people have this standoff in an alley, nobody ever asks, "Where are the police? Why doesn't somebody call the police about all these gunshots?" and that's OK. It's like a blind spot in their logic. So I always thought that what I'd do is someday, when I came up against a blank period in my own writing, I'd turn *The Shotgunners* into a book, since nobody wanted to do it as a movie.

But with *Sleepwalkers* that wasn't a problem. I was really sort of amazed at how much enthusiasm it generated, first at CAA, which agents my stuff, and then with some of the studios when it was making the rounds.

FANG: Do you still see *The Shotgunners* coming together as a novel?

KING: Not in the immediate future, but it's always there. I think the idea's still a good one. At one point it had to do with ghost vigilantes. That was an idea that I had that Peckinpah grabbed onto. But it was basically a story about what went on on a suburban street in Your Town, U.S.A., which is where *Sleepwalkers* is set as well. It's more or less my territory—Your Street, U.S.A., the Great Middlebrow of America.

FANG: There's a ton of movies coming out over the next few months that have your name attached to them in one way or another. Once the film rights are sold, if you're not working on the screenplay, do you tend to disengage yourself?

KING: Yeah.

FANG: Do you always see the films based on your works?

KING: Yeah, at least up to now I have, I think, unless I've missed something somewhere. But back when I was just starting out—this goes back to like 1978, 1979—I'd done my first collection of short stories, *Night Shift*, and there was a bunch of stories from there that got sold to British producer Milton Subotsky. He was at Amicus Productions for a long time; they were Hammer's chief competition at that time and made *Tales from the Crypt* and some other

anthology movies. One of the stories he bought was "The Lawnmower Man." Before Milton died, Dino De Laurentiis bought some of those stories to make his own series of not-very-good movies, including *Sometimes They Come Back*, which was made for TV.

One of the ones that De Laurentiis didn't get was "Lawnmower Man." When Milton Subotsky died, that became part of his estate. So, whoever inherited those rights was able to do whatever they wanted, because the sale was a deal that was done outright by Doubleday. They served as my agent and they didn't give a shit what happened to any of those stories. They didn't make very good deals for me, because they didn't care that much about me, which is one of the reasons why Doubleday isn't my publisher anymore and hasn't participated in anything that's happened since those days. So the moral of that story is that if you misuse the talent, you get screwed in the end.

MICK GARRIS (CENTER) DIRECTED KING AND FELLOW GENRE SCRIBE CLIVE BARKER IN A *Sleepwalkers* CAMEO SEQUENCE.

But regardless of that, it ended up that another company got "The Lawnmower Man" and they did something [interesting] with it. But I didn't even know about the *Lawnmower Man* movie until about three weeks before a poster for it turned up in my local theater.

FANG: What about *Pet Sematary II* and *Children of the Corn II*? Do you have any control over the sequelization of films based on your works?

KING: Sequels are a sore point with me. The way it works, as a general rule, is they'll tell you it's a graven-in-stone thing that a studio won't buy a book to make a movie out of unless you convey sequel rights to them. But it used to be graven in stone, too, that you couldn't sell a book to a publisher unless you gave them an option on your next book, and holes were blasted in that idea a long time ago.

When I sold *Pet Sematary* to Laurel Entertainment to do as a movie with Paramount, [Laurel president] Richard Rubinstein called me on the phone and said, "They won't make this deal without sequel rights." And I said, "I don't want to sell sequel rights to *Pet Sematary*." He gave me the graven-in-stone argument and then said, "Besides, nobody's going to make a sequel to this movie. They won't be able to." Well, anybody who's ever seen a Freddy movie or a *Friday the 13th* movie knows that's crap. You can make a sequel to *anything*. It doesn't necessarily have to make sense, because sense isn't the point. The box office is the point, and even more than the box office, the subsidiary rights are the point—the foreign, videocassette and the cable rights.

So I talked with a guy who was in charge at Paramount at that time and got an equal assurance that no sequel would be made, which was a little bit like President Grant telling the Apaches, "Don't worry, we're going to leave you your native lands." I said OK, and basically we made the deal.

The sequel has now been made. I read the script—or as much of it as I could stand—and I read enough to realize that it was exactly like the first *Pet Sematary* with different characters. I don't approve of the movie and I didn't want it made. I hope that the people who read FANGORIA, the people who read my books and anyone who likes my stuff will stay away from this picture. And this is one film that I will not see.

But it has had this effect, and that is that I will never sell sequel rights to another book to go with movie rights. If somebody wants to make a movie from one of my books, and insist on sequel rights as part of the contract, that book will *not* be sold. The only exception to that is *Sleepwalkers*, because it wasn't a book to begin with, and because it's built in such an openended fashion that—if it were to be a success—people could go on and make as many sequels as they wanted. It's almost like *Dracula* or *Frankenstein*.

FANG: Has there been any film interest in the *Dark Tower* cycle?

KING: Yes, from various places. There's even been one suggestion from a producer in Hollywood to do it as an animated feature—instead of *Fievel Goes West*, this would be *Roland Goes East* [*laughs*]. I said no. There isn't going to be any film of the *Dark Tower* books in my lifetime.

STEPHEN KING LOOKS DOWN THE ROAD AT MANY FUTURE PROJECTS.

CLIVE BARKER'S BOUNDLESS IMAJINATION

BY W.C. STROBY

Although it's mid-August, Clive Barker is fighting off the flu as he sniffs through a phone interview from his Los Angeles home. Though he's left his native Britain to take up residence in Beverly Hills (in a $2-million home once owned by actor Robert Culp), the move to sunnier climes hasn't done much for his health.

But despite his illness, he's determined to go on with the interview. His new book, *Imajica*—an 824-page reworking of the Christ myth set in a universe of parallel worlds known as the Dominions—has just been published by HarperCollins, and he's also struggling to finish a screenplay before embarking on a multicity publicity tour which will take him from Toronto to New York to London and, finally, back to California. Other projects await him there, including a children's fantasy novel, *Everville*, and a proposed film for Universal, *Eden USA*.

In the meantime, other Barker-related projects abound, including British writer/director Bernard (*Paperhouse*) Rose's *Candyman*, an adaptation of Barker's story "The Forbidden" (from Volume Five of the *Books of Blood*) about a supernatural killer who haunts a decrepit housing project. And the successful *Hellraiser III: Hell on Earth* will likely be followed by a *Hellraiser IV*.

Barker himself has made his feature-film acting debut with a cameo in Mick Garris' *Sleepwalkers*. And both Eclipse Books and Marvel's Epic Comics division continue their forays into Barker's works. Epic's slate includes a three-issue adaptation of *Weaveworld* and *Jihad*, a two-part series that pits the Nightbreed against *Hellraiser*'s Cenobites, while Eclipse delivers graphic-novel adaptations of *BOB*'s "Revelations" and "The Yattering and Jack."

But chief on Barker's mind at the moment is *Imajica*, which he hopes will attract a new audience to his work. It's unlike anything Barker has written so far, and ultimately brings us face-to-face with God—here named Hapexamendios. Its hero, an artist and inveterate womanizer known as "Gentle," attempts to reconcile Earth with its four sister worlds and usher in a new age of wonders.

"In terms of its metaphysics, it's certainly the most ambitious piece I've done," Barker claims. "It's as far from being a horror novel as it's possible to get. After all, this is a book in which God appears. The closest I've gotten to the Eternal Throne before has been with angels [in *Weaveworld*]. Now we get to meet the Big Man himself."

Further projects from the author include the second part of *The Art* trilogy, this one featuring Harry D'Amour, Barker's demon-hunting detective from the short stories "The Last Illusion" and "Lost Souls." And then, of course, there are two more sequels to *Cabal*, the last of which, Barker promises, will take his Breed to the Vatican.

BARKER'S CONVERSATION IS STILL TINGED WITH *Nightbreed* REGRETS, BUT HE PLANS ON REVISITING MIDIAN IN THE NEAR FUTURE.

FANGORIA: *Imajica*, because of its complexity, is a book in which most readers are going to see many different things. What would you like to see people bring from it?

CLIVE BARKER: Well, doing a book this scale is as much a dive into a pool of your own subconscious desires and obsessions as anything. I, having just recently surfaced from that book, am only beginning to get a sense of what it contains from people who are coming back to me and saying, "You know, I found this or I found that." So maybe in 10 years' time I can say, "Ah, that's what I was up to."

But at the moment, the book was an attempt to reconfigure a piece of mythology. With *Weaveworld*, the mythology was that of Never-Never Land, how we relate to the idea of the lost world—the place of innocence which we remember from fairy tales— and what would happen if that came back into our lives as adults. In *Imajica*, the subject is the largest myth that the Western world deals with—the Christ story. That means a lot to me, and I wanted to investigate it for new meaning, new significance.

FANG: How long did *Imajica* take you to write?

BARKER: Fourteen months, from the time I first put pen to paper till the day I turned it in. That was writing seven days a week, 14 hours a day—towards the end, it was 16 hours a day.

© 20th Century Fox

But it was always a book which obsessed me, right from the very beginning. I don't quite know yet why that is. Part of it was the fact that the sheer scale of it required total immersion if I was going to pull it off. If I hadn't gotten it right—and I hope I've gotten it at least part right—then I would have looked like a real fool, because here I am dealing with Christ and God and magic and all that stuff.

And when, halfway through the book, the audience realizes that Hapexamendios is the same God that people are worshipping when they go to Sunday Mass, the danger was that the audience would say, "Oh, come on, give me a break. I'll accept the idea of an invented god, but now what you're asking me to accept is that this god is Jehovah, this god is Yahweh, this god is the God whom people worship in the Western world." And that's a very different thing from one of the gods of a [Stephen] Donaldson novel.

FANG: Were you worried at all about alienating a certain area of your readership by publishing a book that's nearly 1,000 pages?

BARKER: There is a danger of alienating [some readers]. I am sure there are going to be people who will say, "Sorry, this is too long." But I also think there's an audience that says, "Give me everything, tell me everything you can tell me." Over the last 40 years there's been a huge and consistent audience for *Lord of the Rings*, and there's certainly a huge audience for the *Dune* books.

I wanted to create my own legends; I wanted to create something that my readership could enter into and invest their time and emotion in and feel deeply about over a period of many days or maybe even weeks, and that would stay with them as a world they could enter and re-experience if they wanted.

FANG: Is this the last of the big books for now?

BARKER: I wish I could say yes. The lazy part of me wishes I could say yes. The last couple of months, I've been thinking that I'm almost obsessed with story. I mean, it's been very strange putting this book down and starting another one right away, and a screenplay. I'm realizing that story really does obsess me. Once I get a story—or the beginnings of one—in my head, it controls me and has to be told.

So there are two more big books—sequels to *The Great and Secret Show*—but neither will be as long as *Imajica*. And I have plots laid—though at great distance; I probably won't get to those for four or five years—for another *Imajica*-scale book, another series of worlds. But these things take a long time to percolate. I can't see myself turning out a book bigger than *Imajica*. But I said that about *The Great and Secret Show*, and look what happened.

FANG: So what's next, writing-wise?

BARKER: I'm delivering to Harper a short children's novel called *Everville*, though it'll have crossover appeal, I hope. And I'm delivering to Universal a screenplay which will be my next project as director. Then I'll come back and write *The Art II*.

FANG: What's the status of your Universal remake of *The Mummy*?

BARKER: *The Mummy* is going into another draft because Mick Garris, who was writing it with me, is making *Sleepwalkers*. So we're checking on other writers to come in on *The Mummy*.

The next film will be a science fiction picture called *Eden USA*, which I've written and will direct, probably sometime early next year. I'll be doing a couple more drafts of the screenplay, and then hopefully we'll just get on and do it. There certainly seems to be enthusiasm at Universal for it, which is good.

FANG: Can you give us any hint as to what it's about?

BARKER: It's fairly top secret at this point. But it's a science fiction/fantasy movie and it's Clive Barker weird [*laughs*].

FANG: What ever happened to the Harry D'Amour film based on ''The Last Illusion''? Is that still viable?

BARKER: Yes, absolutely. In fact, I've just been working on a draft of that. It won't be the next movie to go, but it may very well be the one after that.

FANG: What changed your mind about Hollywood? You were pretty disgusted with the town after *Nightbreed*.

BARKER: Well, it's the place where movies get made. That's the bottom line. And if you want to work in movies, then you just have to be here. There doesn't seem to be any way around it.

As a living environment, there are many things to recommend it; the sun shines and life is relatively easy. But for somebody who ran their movie career, such as it was, from London with an eight-hour time difference between me and the studios, it's very much easier to make an assessment of how your work is being received if you're here amongst the people who are doing the receiving.

The experience of *Nightbreed* and Fox's mismanagement of it were wretched. But it happens to everybody. It will probably happen to me again. It's the way of the world, and the only thing that I could see to help me improve upon the situation was to be here and meet with these people.

FANG: After the disillusionment that

HERE'S ONE CONVENTION WE'D LIKE TO ATTEND: A CONCLAVE OF CENOBITES COMMENCES IN *Jihad* #1.

came with *Nightbreed*'s box-office fail-
ure, do you have any trepidations about
returning to films?

BARKER: Well, of course, you're back
to a collaborative art form. But if I spent
my entire time at my desk writing
novels, I would be a poorer man for it.
Part of my nature is to be somebody
who likes to communicate, likes to work
with other people's ideas. Part of it is
that I still love the cinematic experience
as a viewer. When a movie is fun, when
a movie is good, I can't help thinking,
"Boy, I'd like to be able to do that."
And that desire hasn't gone away.

   And as I say, you look at somebody like David Cronenberg, for instance. After *Nightbreed* came out, he
said to me, "Listen, this is going to happen again. It's happened to me in movie
after movie—people not getting it, critics
hating it and then two years later they
say, "Ah, you know, it wasn't so bad.
It's better than the new movie he's put
out." [*Laughs*]

   In fact, we've seen some interesting reassessments of *Nightbreed*, even in
the recent past. *Entertainment Weekly*
gave an issue over to the "100 Best
Movies That You've Never Heard Of,"
and one of them was *Nightbreed.* It's
doing very well on video.

FANG: What did that experience teach
you? What are your "never again" reso-
lutions as you're preparing *Eden USA*?

BARKER: Well, if it comes down to
naming names, then it's like, "I will
never work with X," you know [*laughs*]?
And I'm always loath to name names.

   But there are a few people whom I
have sworn I would never step into the
same room with again. And they're
mostly The Suits. Inevitably, there are
some individuals who make you think,
"Well, this person screwed me over, and
I'll make sure that I never put myself in
that situation again."

   But in terms of the working proce-
dures, one of the obvious things is that I
will be making a movie in America, in
the same city as my producers, and I am

© Dimension

going to be working much more closely
with them. But who knows how it will
all end up?

   I always go into these things very
optimistically. If you go in cynically, the
work is probably going to suffer. So I go
in there with a smile expecting that,
"Hey, it's going to be transcendentally
wonderful. Prove me wrong."

FANG: Many writers have gone to
Hollywood and have wound up not being worth a damn afterwards, because
they lost whatever it was they had in
the first place. After all, it's a very se-
ductive lifestyle that's nevertheless built
on tradeoffs, concessions and com-
promises. Everybody loves you, everybody tells you you're great. . .

BARKER: Yeah, they love you until
you can't get a table at Spago.

FANG: Does the possibility of losing

**PINHEAD ROARED
OUT OF THE** *Hellraiser*
**FILMS TO BECOME
AN INTERNATIONAL
ICON.**

something of worth—maybe something almost undefinable—by buying into Hollywood bother you?

BARKER: No, it doesn't, and here's why. Firstly, the writers who come to Hollywood tend to come to write screenplays. And then they get beaten and bruised because they don't see their work transferred to the screen in a way that satisfies them, and they end up crying by their swimming pools because the movies don't reflect their vision.

What I'm trying to do as a writer/director is hold to my vision a little bit more. We all know that you don't hold onto your vision 100 percent, because there are too many pressures on you—commercial pressures, producers' pressures, whatever. But I have more of a chance at keeping my vision intact because I'm coming in as both a writer and director.

And the other thing is that the bad experiences of *Nightbreed* drove me back into the arms of the written word with more fervor for it than ever before. And if *Imajica* sounds like an imaginative cry from the heart—that this is a world which is entirely mine, nobody can tread on it—it's because of that very fact.

But I've always seen moviemaking and writing as complementary skills and complementary endeavors. I'm not even changing genres, really. I'm writing in the *fantastique* and I'm making movies in the *fantastique*, and would hope to continue to do both.

FANG: Writing-wise, how far in the future are the next two installments of the *Cabal* trilogy?

BARKER: Well, they're responsibilities, that's what they are. This is what I was saying before about having these stories in my head. I know what I want to write, I know what happens in them, I just . . . who has time? These are books which have to be written and I know it. And I will finish them.

After *Everville* and the movie, the next one will almost certainly be *The Art II*, in preference to the second *Cabal/*

Nightbreed book, simply because the audience for *The Great and Secret Show* was so enormous worldwide. In fact, that book is in more languages now than any others of mine. And that's an audience to which I want to tell the rest of that story. I want to tell the rest of the Nightbreed story as well, but at least I know the comic books are taking over in the meantime.

FANG: Are the comic stories overlapping with your ideas for where the Nightbreed story is going?

BARKER: No, not at all. If they ever did, I'd tell them not to run them. But my ideas for where *Nightbreed II* and *III* are going are so wild that I don't think comic books could do it anyway. I'm very much watching over that and making sure that, while the *Nightbreed* characters can run riot on the pages of Epic Comics for awhile, the way that they will run riot when I actually start to write about them again will be something completely different.

FANG: How involved have you been so far with the comic adaptations?

BARKER: I think of myself as a benign godfather—I visit them at their christening and I send presents every birthday [*laughs*]. They run the artists past me and tell me how the storylines are going to go, and we meet every now and then. When I'm in New York, I always call in and have some conferences with [Marvel]. With Eclipse Comics, it's exactly the same thing.

So while I don't have day-to-day, hands-on control, they always know that if they need me for a piece of mythology or something like that, I will be around. Generally speaking, they've done good jobs. The comics have been well-done and intelligently handled, and I feel that the spirit of Clive Barker hasn't been significantly compromised in those things. Far from it. I mean, *Jihad* will blow your socks off. It is amazing. Beautiful artwork by Paul Johnson, beautiful writing by Dan Chichester. Really tremendous work.

FANG: How did your cameo in *Sleep-walkers* come about?

BARKER: Steve King and Mick Garris had asked me to do it. I have a scene with Steve and Tobe Hooper. Well, not a scene actually, more like a shot [*laughs*]. But never mind, I enjoyed it.

It was just great fun. Joe Dante is in it, and John Landis. Steve is playing a graveyard owner, and Tobe and I play forensics men and we both get blood on our hands. I would have liked to have come to a terrible end. Either that or been involved in an X-rated sex scene, but if I couldn't have either of those, I guess being in a scene with Steve and Tobe is the next best thing.

FANG: Was *Hellraiser III* based on your story treatment?

BARKER: No, it's all fresh. It's a story by Tony Randel and Pete Atkins, and obviously a screenplay by Pete, though I don't know how much of Tony's contribution to the original story was included, since Tony Hickox came in. Certainly it's a Pinhead movie, which is the right decision, and Doug Bradley has a lot to do with it.

FANG: How much input did you have on Bernard Rose's *Candyman*?

BARKER: I'm executive producer, but it's his baby.

FANG: Were you involved with the writing at all?

BARKER: No, it's Bernard's work, he's writer and director. I watched over it, again as a benign godfather, and he's done a fine job of adapting it. It's a scary tale.

FANG: Do you miss Britain?

BARKER: No, I don't. I miss seeing my parents, I miss seeing my friends sometimes, but there's been lots going on here and I'm pretty satisfied with how things are progressing. I'm hugely enjoying being here in the U.S. and making new friends and being close to the heart of the filmmaking business.

FANG: You've accomplished a great deal of work in a relatively short time. It's fair to say you're driven, to a certain

extent. I don't think you'd disagree. . .

BARKER: No, I wouldn't disagree with that.

FANG: . . .and I'm sure you've made sacrifices, personal and otherwise, in order to do the amount of work you've done in the amount of time you have. Approaching 40, are you happy with what you've accomplished so far, midway through your life?

BARKER: No. The moment you're satisfied is probably the moment you lay down the pen. There are huge numbers of things I want to achieve which I haven't come near achieving, private agendas you think about and hopefully come closer to as time goes by.

I am *absolutely* driven. But I am driven not so much by the idea of having huge amounts of money, or going on *Arsenio Hall*, as by the idea of telling these tales. The tales drive me.

When I was in the middle of writing *Imajica*, I would get up and go to my desk at 8 a.m. and I would finish maybe at 9 at night, and then I would dream about the book—and that would be my life. And I was *happy*. That's what's important, I was happy doing that. And people would say, "Oh wait, you haven't been out, you haven't had a social evening out, you haven't gone to dinner or whatever for months, what's wrong with you, are you sick?" And I'd say, "No, I'm really happy. I'm telling the story, I'm writing the book, I'm happy."

So I don't look to the grand plan, the overview, too often, because it would make me crazy. But when I do, I think, boy, I've still got a huge amount to do.

FANG: You're about to embark on another publicity tour—lots of cities, lots of different people, interviews, talk shows, signings, etc. Does it take you away from your work? Or is there a part of you that really loves it?

BARKER: I absolutely enjoy the process of bringing what I have done out to the world and saying, "This is what I

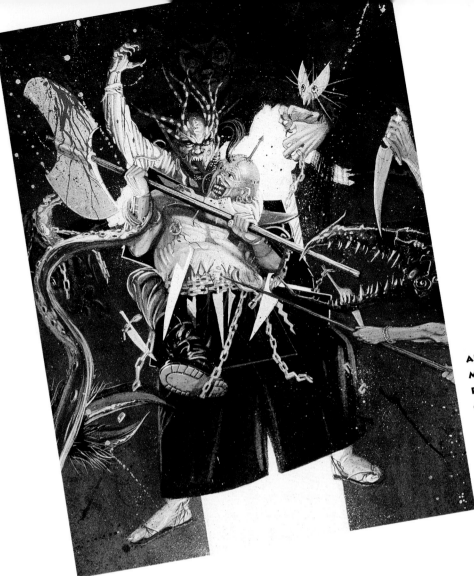

AND MAY THE BEAST MAN WIN! PELOQUIN VS. NEW CENOBITE ALASTOR IN THE SECOND ISSUE OF *Jihad*.

did, guys.'' I don't understand authors who feel resentful meeting their fans or don't want to shake their hands. I mean, that's what your primary relationship is, that's what you're doing this for. A book is dead until it's read. A movie is dead until it's seen. It doesn't exist. What use is a book that isn't read?

But I've had some experiences on the road which have been fairly mind-blowing in some ways, like finding my-self on a fundamentalist radio station because I'd been misbooked [*laughs*]. That happened to me once in the Deep South. Suddenly I'm sitting there and I'm thinking, ''Why are there all these crosses around the studio?'' And I real-ized I was on a fundamentalist station, and it was like, ''Today's sacrificial victim for the fundamentalist phone-in will be

Clive Barker'' [*laughs*].

Those things have happened. They're part of the texture of it. But yes, find me in the middle of the tour on a gloomy afternoon and ask me again and you might hear a gnashing of teeth over the phone, or when I'm on another talk show with a host who doesn't know anything about me who asks me where I get my ideas from. Sometimes that makes me crazy.

But I am very proud of and excited by *Imajica*. My readers are going to be excited by it. It is part of my job, part of my work, to go out there and talk about it and have as many people as possible put out their 20 bucks to buy it. That's something that comes with the territory, and I'm not about to turn away from that.

THE MANY MUTATIONS OF "ALIEN³"

BY DANIEL SCHWEIGER

COMPLEX ROD PUPPETS AUGMENTED THE MAN-IN-A-SUIT ACTION TO BRING *Alien³*'S CREATURE TO LIFE.

The plot is as old as horror itself: A lone female is chased through a haunted house, an unspeakable evil just behind her. Not even God hears the woman's prayers, leaving the heroine with only her wits against pure evil.

No film made better use of this scenario than 1979's *Alien*, revamping the mansion into the industrialized confines of a futuristic spaceship, its sexy protagonist now liberated with guts and a flame gun. This claustrophobic setting was expanded for the even more popular *Aliens*, which multiplied the creatures into explosive horror action. But now *Alien³* has returned to the original's Gothic atmosphere with a vengeance, making it perfect for the nihilistic '90s.

Alien³ begins as a facehugger causes the sleep chamber containing Ripley (Sigourney Weaver) and the other survivors to eject from the space cruiser *Sulaco*. It crash-lands onto the toxic prison planet of Fiorine, with Ripley the only survivor; she soon finds herself shaved bald and surrounded by hostile inmates. When a surviving hugger attaches itself to a rottweiler, the most bloodthirsty extraterrestrial yet is hatched to terrorize "Fury 1."

Alien³'s greatest fight for survival, however, was waged by Alec Gillis and Tom Woodruff Jr., the FX engineers who were terrorized by a mutating script, pressured by a perfectionist director and nearly eviscerated when some of their most unusual creations were tossed out of the studio's airlock. Yet the forces behind Amalgamated Dynamics have emerged triumphant after their fight with the beast, adding their grotesque vision to the revolutionary Alien designs of H.R. Giger. Most importantly, Gillis and Woodruff have accomplished their work with little help from mentor Stan Winston, moving out from under his shadow as creature coordinators on *Aliens* to FX supervisors for this sequel.

Woodruff and Gillis first met while under Winston's tutelage, their talents and responsibilities maturing through such creature-heavy projects as *Invaders from Mars*, *The Monster Squad* and *The Terminator*. "Stan delegates a lot of responsibility to his key people, but the effects always remained his," Woodruff comments. "As coordinators, Alec and I were always designing 'gags,' like Bishop getting torn in half for *Aliens*. We were happy to work under Stan, and the only reason we parted company was that he scaled down operations to concentrate on effects for his own films."

Woodruff would play the Alien-inspired *Pumpkinhead* in Winston's moviemaking debut, the bony creature co-piloted by shop members Gillis, John Rosengrant, Shane Mahan and Richard Landon while their boss concentrated on the film's twilight mood and frenzied acting. Woodruff and Gillis' last collaboration with Winston would be *Leviathan*'s hastily glimpsed sea monster. "It was good timing for us to leave," Gillis says, "and we parted with Stan's blessings. He'll always be our mentor, and he sometimes recommends us for jobs."

Setting up their FX warehouse in Chatsworth, CA, Gillis and Woodruff received their baptism by sand on *Tremors*. Ron Underwood's retro-horror comedy would prove to be their most demanding film, with the pair designing giant, carnivorous earthworms in both full-scale and miniature editions. The film became a hit among genre fans and established Woodruff and Gillis as FX newcomers who could do the job right.

While work on *Tales from the Crypt* and *The Grifters* quickly followed, Winston's commitments would land Woodruff and Gillis their biggest assignment. With his fabrications for *Terminator 2* and *Predator 2* making him unable to take on *Alien³*, Winston and producer Gale Anne Hurd helped to get Gillis and Woodruff on the show. Now

DENTAL HYGIENE IS
A NECESSITY AT THE
FX SHOP.

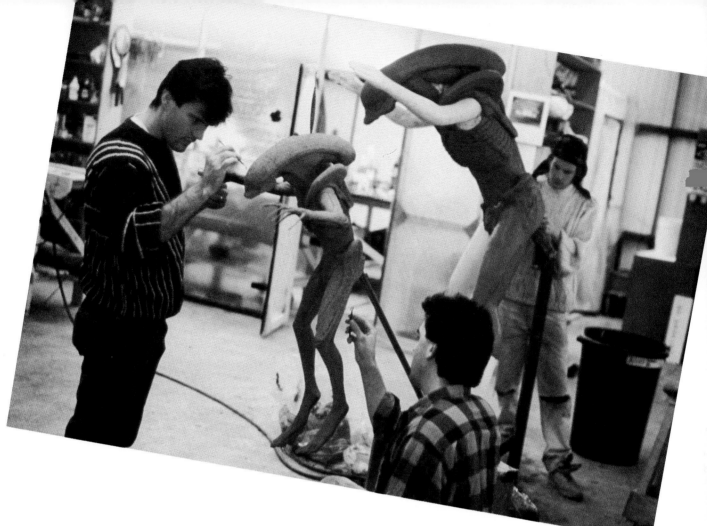

ALEC GILLIS (RIGHT) AND TOM WOODRUFF JR. BEGIN SCULPTING THEIR LITHELY-DESIGNED CREATURES.

they were solely responsible for the Alien FX, even though the film's game of musical scripters hadn't finalized the Alien's abilities. "I've been in this business for 12 years, while Tom's been in it for 10," Gillis says. "*Alien³* isn't a new thing for us, but it's still exciting to be working on this kind of high-profile movie. You go into it with enthusiasm instead of fear.

"It would have been an obvious approach to turn *Alien³* into a gigantic action picture," Gillis continues. "One script used a 'king' Alien, while another had radio-controlled power loaders fighting an army of Queens. But there were practical considerations against making a $150-million movie, because the story's hook is dangling the threat of the Aliens getting to Earth. The sequel ideas were like the difference between *Psycho* and *Zulu*! *Alien³* finally went with a script that got back to the original's mood and suspense. It's harsh, brutal and dark, very daring for a big-money sequel."

Winston had been responsible for juggling the FX budget on *Aliens*, and now Woodruff and Gillis had to prove they could save money for Fox as the studio changed directors (from Vincent Ward to David Fincher) and writers. Once again basing their creature shop in England, Woodruff and Gillis began making Alien victims in July 1990. However, they still had no idea about the monster's appearance until the end of November, and this confusion prolonged their six-month stay on *Alien³* to 40 weeks.

"We pride ourselves on being flexible enough to look at a film artistically, but also to see it from a business point of view, and know that there are certain limitations," Woodruff remarks. "The production shifted into neutral because of the rewrites, and we decided to stay in England instead of shipping everyone home for a month or two. Since every day was eating up money, we kept building corpses, which aren't the main thrust of effects work. A lot of people would say, 'To hell with this situation. Send me home and call me up later!' But you can't do that when you're working in

© 20th Century Fox

this industry. Though Fox would tell us the Alien had to do certain things, it's odd to think we spent all that time to build it. There isn't 10 months of work in that Alien."

THAT'S NOT HUMPTY DUMPTY ON TOP OF THE WALL.

Body construction would allow Woodruff and Gillis more time to flesh out their Alien designs. While the creatures' insectoid appearances had become as instantly recognizable as Jason's hockey mask, the FX men were still determined to add their imaginations to Giger's chrome-plated jaws. "You're working with set parameters on a sequel, so there isn't a whole lot of flexing your design muscles," Woodruff confides. "But ever since *Alien* came out, people have misinterpreted the 'biomechanical' style. They think it's a monster with tubes and cardboard stuck all over it. That's only a construction technique that Giger used when he sculpted for the first movie. We even had one of his original creatures for reference on *Aliens*, and it literally had plastic parts that you could read the catalog numbers off of! We wanted the monsters in *Alien³* to look like they were growing into a mechanical being."

"Even *Alien* wasn't completely true to Giger's vision," Gillis says. "I don't mean to be pompous, but his own suit wasn't accurate to his paintings. Our goal was to sculpt Giger's designs into repeating organic textures, almost like deer antlers. We also put more color into the Alien, which was originally just black and sepia. Since the effects of *Alien³* wouldn't have the spectacle of the last film, we wanted to make this creature into a believable organism."

"This is still Giger's Alien, and we've done very little to change it," Woodruff insists. "In fact, we were breaking out his *Necronomicon* at the finishing stages, since this monster would be scrutinized more than ever. *Aliens'* theatrical lighting turned them into moving textures. This beast is animalistic instead of insectlike, since it's gestated inside a rottweiler. The Alien's picked up the dog's instincts, and can run around on all fours."

During the even more tortured birth of *Alien³*'s plot, the facehugger was originally seen latching onto an ox, its chestburster hatching in a meat locker. Realizing that audiences might expect an Alien with udders, this concept was quickly scrapped. "Fox never had a problem with coming back and saying, 'Sorry, guys. We know you've built these things, but there's a new direction, and we're not going to use them,' " Gillis sighs. "We had to keep ourselves and the crew morally afloat, because people put their blood, sweat and tears into the stuff, and have a tendency to get upset when an effect's cancelled. There were six stages of Aliens, count 'em! But we're not griping about the script changes, because any story should constantly be honed. That only shows us the film's getting better, and if the effect doesn't serve the plot, then there's no reason for it."

The most conceptually interesting stage is the "Bambi-burster," a puppylike creature that jumps out of the rottweiler's chest and scampers across the floor. "David Fincher thought it would be more sleek if the monster came out of a dog, and the rottweiler is a pretty brutal animal to start with," Woodruff reveals. "David needed something that could walk and be photographed from every angle, which made him think about putting a dog in a suit to supplement a cable-controlled puppet. That seemed like a pretty dumb notion at first, but the more we thought about it, the better his idea sounded."

Since this weird chestburster needed to be done with appliance makeup, Woodruff ended up going from a greyhound to a whippet for the thinnest canine possible. Using a life sculpture, the technicians constructed a creation of spandex and foam pieces, including a head that was covered with slime and blood, all to make the animal resemble their mechanical effect. "The whippet looked great, but it wouldn't perform on the set," Woodruff says. "We couldn't even get it to trot down the hall, which was all it had to do! So I ended up sliding the dog into the shot."

Gillis and Woodruff's most novel contribution to the Alien evolutionary chain is a shocking discovery made by Ripley when she scans her own body: a chestburster embryo. This puppet was placed inside an anatomically correct Ripley mockup, with four cutaway sections to be shot with motion-control passes. "The images were then transferred to video, so the effect would be like looking through Sigourney Weaver's body," Woodruff explains. "We even had her heart pumping at one stage. The embryo was made out of translucent urethane, and lit from behind. That gave it a glow that revealed the creature's nervous system, including its beating heart. We took the chestburster's design and worked backwards, accentuating the head while making the arms and legs smaller."

As Ripley engages in a fight to the finish with the mature being and the one wrapped around her innards, Gillis and Woodruff devoted most of their attention to the Alien's skin instead of its jaw-popping trickery. "There's nothing novel about our construction," Gillis admits. "This is a rubber-suit kind of thing, but we have gadgets that make it better than what the average Joe is doing. There's a mechanical head, tail and movable thumbs, but the strength of our Alien is always in its appearance."

The "adolescent" Alien makes its terrifying entrance to spit acid from a ventilation shaft. This quickly glimpsed puppet was one of Alien³'s nods to its forebear, equipped with a translucent dome and double jaws. Cables would pull back its fangs, while a plastic tube spewed the flesh-dissolving puke.

When it came time for the Alien to suit up, Gillis was insistent that Woodruff should play the monster instead of a taller actor. "This is a believable creature instead of a stylized nightmare, which made it important for Tom to play the monster," Gillis explains. "The actor in Alien had great proportion but you never had the feeling that he was a performer. That monster's success was due to the fast cuts and obtuse angles that Ridley Scott used, while the warriors in Aliens were all stuntmen. But after playing every creature from Pumpkinhead to the Gill Man, Tom had more experience in suits than just about anyone. He knows exactly what his body's doing in a rubber costume, and can go for 14 hours without having to go to the bathroom. I've never met anyone who could do that!"

Though *Alien³* generates its terror from the beast's vicious and unexpected attacks, Gillis and Woodruff needed to provide the monster with its "Method." "We wanted to avoid giving the Alien human traits, because this is a life form that's just doing its job of killing and procreating," Gillis explains. "The fact that the Alien terrifies the shit out of people is a byproduct of its actions. In nature, all behavior is controlled by intelligence or instinct. But this creature's instincts are pumped to such a high level, they become their own kind of intelligence.

"Some of the early drafts had the Alien tearing a guy in half, and then dramatically tossing the head at someone's feet. But that's pure bravado. Now the Alien walks right up to Ripley after murdering a person in front of her. It's deciding whether to kill her or not, but scurries off upon realizing that Ripley's carrying the embryo. If you watched that scene from the human point of view, you'd say the Alien's just killed Ripley's lover, and is sticking out its jaws like a kind of laugh. But that's the character we put into the Alien, getting across the fear of a wild animal."

"The Alien had to be threatening in every encounter with Ripley, yet pull back at the last minute," Woodruff adds. "You have to thrill people by making them think she's in danger, and that's difficult to get across when I'm wearing a fiberglass head! The infirmary scene, when the Alien's tongue caresses her cheek, gives us the best clue about their relationship."

With Fincher's career built on MTV and Madonna, Gillis and Woodruff were apprehensive about whether this 27-year-old wunderkind would obscure their work with his visual fetishes. "When we asked who he was, some people said, 'It's David Fincher, king of the pop videos!' So we thought, 'Oh no! Another flash-and-trash kid!'" Gillis remarks. "But the more we worked with him, it became apparent that David's extravagance only showed that he wanted the highest-quality work. Since we like to push our effects to the max when everyone else is telling us to make things simpler, it was great to have someone who would push us!"

The movie that Fincher wanted would be uncompromisingly bleak, a rude shock to audiences who were used to seeing Ripley blow away any Alien threat. With the savage script virtually being written as the film was made, Fincher's attention to every minute detail and his slap at happy-ending horror would unleash a storm of negative publicity. Yet Gillis and Woodruff would stick by their auteur, even manufacturing an Alien suit for him to wear on set. "David was very demanding, because he knew the audience would be cheated if our effects were cut too much," Gillis concludes. "He needed to see the Alien's actions occur in real time, without using stuff like reverse photography or undercranking. David wanted *Alien³*'s reality to exist beyond the film, and that would be our toughest challenge."

REINVENTING GREMLINS

BY BILL WARREN

I've done puppet things before,'' Rick Baker admits, ''though mainly I've done them with people inside. But I've always wanted to do something like this, where it's all mechanical or puppet creatures.''

This ''something'' is *Gremlins 2: The New Batch*, the Joe Dante/Charlie Haas/Rick Baker miniature monster extravaganza, for which the FX budget alone was reportedly $1 million more than the entire budget of the first movie.

After producer Mike Finnell and Joe Dante had convinced Baker to at least think about it, ''I finally talked to them again,'' Baker recounts. ''If I could change stuff, if I could change what the Gremlins are, keep them in the ballpark but make them neater, if I could make characters instead of them all being the same, if something could be written so they would be specific characters, I'd be more interested.''

Baker knew that he would need an enormous crew (eventually, nearly 80 people worked for him on the movie), and would therefore require a much larger building. He fretted about looking for another place, and the problems of having two separate locales. ''One day I came to work and saw a sign on the building next door that said 'For Lease.' I thought maybe this was an omen that I should do this movie—you can't get more convenient than that.''

Baker is now almost certainly the most famous makeup artist in the world, something he finds ''very strange'' to think about. ''I don't think that I'm that different a person from when I was 16 years old and wanted to do this. I'm not as shy, but I still like what I'm doing—I'm still a fan of this kind of movie. I'm amazed when somebody knows who I am, when I'm introduced and they go, '*The* Rick Baker?!' and get excited about meeting me. I always hoped I would be considered one of the best artists, and I

FX MASTER RICK BAKER TOSSED UP A VEGETABLE GREMLIN IN *The New Batch*.

guess I am. It's a neat feeling, but with it comes responsibility. I feel pressure to maintain the quality of my work."

The quality has been high enough for Baker to win two Academy Awards, including the very first ever given in competition for his work on John Landis' landmark *An American Werewolf in London* (1981), and another for *Harry and the Hendersons* (1987). Winning the award felt "great, and frightening," Baker admits. "I thought that after you went through the terror of going up there and getting it, you'd just go back to your seat. I didn't realize you went through this whole paparazzi thing, all these interviews and stuff, and I was totally unprepared. I'd said that I had always hoped that someday I would win an Oscar, then realized that they didn't give Oscars for what I do. The funny thing is, they *don't* give Oscars for what I do now. They've eliminated the type of work I do, which is things with mechanics, from the awards."

Baker must be around 43 by now, but despite the gray in his hair, he's not just youthful, he's positively boyish. His face is unlined, his manner is both shy and confident and he frequently uses words like "stuff" and "neat." When he talks, he has little conversations between himself and people in his past, laughing a lot as he does so. Even his laugh is shy and youthful, as if he's afraid someone will overhear him and tell him to get serious about his work.

He's *very* serious about his work, but it's also his play. He's a man who's doing exactly what he wants to do; he's arguably the best there is at what he does, and he makes a great deal of money doing it. Rick Baker is a genuinely happy man—something like being cut out of the makeup Oscar race is almost a side issue. To him, the

LEFT
THE GREAT MAN HIMSELF READIES ONE OF HIS CABLE-CONTROLLED GREMLIN PUPPETS.

RIGHT
THE BRAIN GREMLIN GIVES HIS NEW MOVIE TWO CLAWS UP.

All *Gremlins* photos © Warner Bros.

joy comes from being able to make monsters for a living. The first article ever written on Baker was "Rick Baker, Monster Maker" in an old issue of *Famous Monsters of Filmland*, and that could be the title of *any* article on him even today. Which is the way he wants it.

Baker's shop, which fills most of the building, is quiet now, with some of the gremlins on display; it must have been a madhouse at the peak of production of *Gremlins 2*. Among the ideas that they didn't get to try were several gags in the genetics lab sequence, such as an elephant gremlin who's frightened by a mouse gremlin, and beats it to death with another gremlin. Or the werewolf gremlin that was a pet idea of Baker's, because of his and Dante's connections with major werewolf movies. "I wanted to have a shot-for-shot thing like that; a gremlin drinks some stuff, holds up his hand, and goes through the change. I wanted to do a tribute to monster movies, a whole mad lab deal—a Frankenstein one, for example—but things got cut way down. It's still enormous, an awful lot of work, but it was even bigger when we first started talking about it."

Baker admits, "I don't think there was anything all that innovative" about the work he and his giant crew did on *Gremlins 2*. "I suppose I could be a real bullshitter like a lot of guys are, and there are some things we did that a normal person would consider real innovative, but the hardest thing about this job was the amount. There was so much to make.

"Although I don't think there's really anything new in the techniques we used, it is done better than it has ever been done before, for the same type of work. What I enjoy about my job is getting to make these toys—it's fun. I am able to make things I could never make on my own—I couldn't *afford* to!" he laughs. "With *Gremlins 2*, I was able to try a lot of things I'd always wanted to do. Some of them had been done before, but I had wanted to do them *before* they had been done before!"

The project on which he had wanted to do them was the aborted *Night Skies*, the movie that Steven Spielberg cancelled in favor of *E.T. The Extra-Terrestrial*. "We did a lot of things in this film that I was hoping to do in *Night Skies*," Baker reveals. "I still don't understand what happened exactly on *Night Skies*. I sent Steven a tape of a prototype thing I did that he raved about. We went ahead and started making all this stuff, and he came in one day and said that he didn't want to make the movie." Since Baker *did*, and found it hard to transfer his enthusiasm from *Night Skies* to the *E.T.* project, Spielberg angrily locked Baker out of the lab.

"Before I did *Harry and the Hendersons*, I had to talk to Steven, because I still had a problem working with him. I wanted to know what happened. I thought I had done some good, innovative work, and got bad-mouthed for it. I talked to Steven, and we decided we both made mistakes, but were both older and wiser now, so we went ahead." And they've had no problems since.

Because Baker had to oversee the entire *Gremlins 2* project, he had to turn over the sculpting chores to artists he trusted. For the "generic" gremlins, those other than the five lead gremlins (including Gizmo), Steve Wang and Matt Rose each sculpted a prototype; these two were manufactured en masse, and about half of each batch were painted brown, the other half green, giving in effect four types of gremlins: Green Steves, Green Matts, Brown Matts and Brown Steves.

The Matt Gremlin, Baker says, "is really close to my original painting of what the generic gremlin should be. Matt's great—besides being very talented, he's a very dedicated and hard, hard worker. He's done an amazing amount of work on this film. Steve Wang did the spider gremlin, and Mohawk before he's a spider. I did a rough sketch, Matt did a little maquette and Steve did the final work, which I thought was great." For those of you keeping score, Steve Gremlins have a flatter face and bulgier eyes than the Matt Gremlins, and look somewhat monkeylike, while the Matt Gremlins are more lizardy.

The techniques used to animate the little monsters are pretty much the same as in the first film, including push-pull cables operated by joysticks, radio-operated faces, operating wires going into the gremlins' feet and poles that come out of their backs. There are hand-puppet gremlins for mass crowd scenes, and even gremlins mounted on football helmets for scenes in which they scuttle by the camera.

The difference between Chris Walas' work in *Gremlins* and that of Baker in *Gremlins 2* isn't the mechanics—it's the sheer mass of gremlinosity. As FX assistant Bart Mixon points out, "Each character has at least four versions: close-up puppets with puppeteered arms, while the faces are electronically controlled with joysticks; puppets that don't have so much for the face, just blinks and ear movements; then we have hand-puppet versions with no arm mechanics, so each character has at least four versions. There are the four main characters, then four generic characters, so that's eight, then we start getting into the mutations, so just for these guys, there are about 20 or 30 puppets total. For the background gremlins, we made 175 puppets for the big crowd scenes. There are a *lot* of puppets."

And when multiplied by photographic mattes, there are even more; in one shot, you can see about 1,000 gremlins!

"With Gizmo," Mixon explains, "we made about 10 different puppets. For some, we had an electronic cable that plugs into part of the control. That goes to a box that feeds off more electronic lines that go to the joy sticks, so that instead of doing this

BORROWING INSPIRATION (AND SOME DNA) FROM A FELLOW LAB SPECIMEN, ONE CREATURE BECOMES THE BAT GREMLIN (ABOVE).

with radio controls, where you're afraid of interference with more than one puppet, it all goes directly into the puppet so you don't worry about signals bouncing off." In one scene, all five mogwais were working, which required 30 puppeteers.

Mixon uncrates one of the close-up gremlins, which operates from a bar that goes into the back, and manipulates the controls, making the gremlin's arm move. He also demonstrates the flying bat gremlin, which hangs from an elevated platform with a seat. Doug Beswick did the stop-motion scenes of the spider and bat gremlins. "In addition to the stop-motion bat gremlin, we made this one for close-ups, like when it claws at Dick Miller," Mixon explains. "We have a puppeteer who lies on his stomach, and operates the wings with rods. Another sits up above and works the legs, with more controls. This whole thing can be suspended from a crane; they had it about 20 or 30 feet in the air."

The Lenny mogwai was originally set to transform into the Brain Gremlin (with the voice of Tony Randall) after swallowing some stuff in the genetics lab, but Dante opted to go with a generic gremlin, which created a few problems. Lenny's lips had been designed for human speech, and the lizard-mouthed generic gremlin's certainly had not. A method called, improbably, the Gilderfluke system was employed: The lips of the gremlin were computer-operated, so that the exact same lip-sync could be achieved with each scene. "The problem was," explains Baker, "that Tony Randall spoke really quickly. I thought we would have to undercrank it, because I didn't think the servo motors would keep up with how fast the lips had to move. As it turned out, they did, and we didn't have to undercrank anything. All in all, it worked very well."

Not only is there more stop-motion in *Gremlins 2* than in the first film, but there is some blue-screen work with Gizmo, which wasn't done at all in the first picture. There's also an odd, optically manufactured scene with Christopher Lee and Gizmo. Dennis Michelson created the movie's optical FX.

There are 65 opticals in the film, Michelson relates. "Almost half of them are of the electric gremlin, and in the finale. It's straight, two-or-three-level cel animation, with electrical bolts being rotoscoped in, frame by frame. There's nothing terribly ground-breaking here; you do a certain amount of R&D to get the look." The cel animation is by Mauro Maressa and Kevin Kutchaver.

Back in his office, Baker again says that it wasn't the novelty of the FX that was the hard part of *Gremlins 2*—it was the project's scale. The most rewarding thing for Baker was "just to have done it. To have survived the job. And the fact that I didn't go insane during it. Many of the crew said they had never enjoyed working on a picture so much. I found that very satisfying."

As for Baker himself, "I liked working with Joe—and what I liked about it was that he's really open to suggestions. In fact, he likes them, which is kind of rare. I have to say that it really was a good experience. I was worried about all the artistic egos being a headache, but everybody got along swell. I had a great crew, very talented and easygoing."

However, even after 20 years working in special FX, Baker still grins ruefully as he says, "It's a strange business, this moviemaking business, and you can quote me on that."

"TERMINATOR 2"— COMPUTER HACKER

BY ANTHONY C. FERRANTE

Terminator 2's **MORPHING VILLAIN USHERED IN A NEW AGE OF MOTION PICTURE FX.**

In the not-so-distant future of *Terminator 2: Judgment Day*, machines wage war against mankind in a postnuclear landscape of charred freeways and scorched playgrounds. Although *T2* presents a cautionary tale about society losing touch with its humanity, relying more on computers and machines to govern and control the future, the film would ironically not have been the landmark event it was without a little electronic assistance.

Dennis Muren, Industrial Light & Magic's senior visual FX supervisor, was in charge of bringing *T2*'s state-of-the-art, groundbreaking computer-generated visuals to the screen, thus allowing Robert Patrick's T-1000 to ooze to life in the film's most memorable moments. Technology may be one of the film's villains, but it is also the movie's star.

"Before the movie's release, everybody was writing about the financial risk—the real risk was if the effects were going to work," explains Larry Kasanoff, head of Lightstorm Entertainment.

Though comprising approximately six minutes of screen time and only around 50 of the film's 150 visual FX shots, the T-1000's metallic morphing scenes required nearly 40 computer animators to execute and operate ILM's Silicon Graphics computers (ILM owns the biggest computer animation facility in the world), as well as the creation and designing of custom-made software. With two months of preproduction and eight months of work, the final product eventually used over 60 gigabytes of computer memory and, according to Kasanoff, amazingly came in under budget. Though no actual figures have been disclosed, Kasanoff hints that "the special effects budget was more than the entire cost of the first *Terminator*."

"We needed the best of everything that could be supplied—the best people, the best producers, the best technicians and the best art directors," explains Steve Williams, senior computer graphics animator. "Given the amount of equipment we bought, it was the most productive show ILM has ever done. We came in ahead of schedule and under budget, so that was really gratifying to the upper management in terms of future productions of this magnitude."

"Digital filmmaking" is what assistant visual FX supervisor Mark Dippé calls this new method of manipulating film via computer to create images beyond the capabilities of existing film technology. And although, according to Dippé, varied methods of computer filmmaking have been around since the '60s, along with a few attempts in the '80s to fully integrate live action with computer animation (*TRON* and *The Last Starfighter*), it wasn't until director James Cameron's *The Abyss* and *T2* that the two processes got the believable integration they deserved.

"It allows you to do things much more freely and flexibly," Dippé asserts. "Normally when you go out on a set, you shoot footage, you come back and all your takes are screwed up, and you only have a couple that work and you're stuck with them. With the computer, you're much freer to do almost anything to the picture. You can de-blur it. You can add more red to it. You can cut one character out and put another one in. You can add a whole new element you were missing in the original photography, like a car flying through the sky. You can change the lighting so it looks like sunset. You don't have to worry about things like using light when shooting exteriors. Basically, you can manipulate things as far as you want."

This manipulation of the image is central to the believability of the T-1000 character. Made of liquid metal (mimetic polyalloy is the Cameron-coined term), he is a streamlined, advanced Terminator. He doesn't need the physique and muscular build of the older T-800 Arnold Schwarzenegger model to be destructive and efficient. The T-1000's mechanism allows him to immediately regenerate himself when he's shot at, change into any person he comes into contact with and assimilate himself into any

ARNOLD FINDS OUT THAT HIS NEW, IMPROVED FOE ISN'T SO EASILY TERMINATED.

solid shape or object, as long as it's of equal size and isn't complex machinery.

"Basically, Stan Winston did most of the prosthetics, animatronics and puppet work, and we did all the sequences that required a transformation or changes in shape," Dippé explains. "Sculptures, puppets and animatronic work can only do so much, so for the very fluid metamorphosing sequences, that's where the computer animation comes in."

The first stages of creating the T-1000 regenerations began early in the preproduction phase. Actor Robert Patrick was brought to ILM's Marin County facilities, where his body was photographed from head to toe, allowing the FX crew to study the shape of his body and how it would move during the course of the film, whether he was running, raising his fists or swinging his arms. Next, this photographic material was fed into a specialized computer, where a CG (computer-generated) Robert Patrick was composed that could walk, move and run exactly like the actor.

"My job was to test and build his body, and try to get him to work correctly for the film," details Williams. "What that meant was that we had to build him in four separate stages: a smooth stage all the way to a fully clothed with gun belt stage. Then they were supplied to different teams."

The sequence that defined the project for Dippé was the moment when the Silver Surfer-looking T-1000 walks out of the flaming truck explosion and transforms himself back into a man. "There's a rule of thumb in special effects: When you see the first big shot, you have to sell the audience on that," says Dippé. "If you don't, you've blown the rest of them, because they won't believe it. When we built our own walking man, that was the cornerstone of the project. Once we went through that process, we had developed our look and basic technique, and we had accomplished the toughest scene in the movie."

Since neither a puppet nor a real man could achieve this feat, computer technology filled those huge shoes. In addition, digital filmmaking picks up the slack where traditional blue screen, which sometimes reveals matte lines around an object or actor,

All Terminator photos © TriStar

usually ends up looking fake. Williams explains that this kind of compositing also results in a higher resolution. "In the old days, it would have involved combining foreground and background elements, so that you ended up with possibly two to three generations of film. We can get away with doing it in one generation."

The next phase consisted of integrating the live-action photography and CG animation. Dippé describes it as being much like the haunted house effect at Disneyland, where live-action photography is projected onto three-dimensional models. "This is called mksticky (pronounced "make-sticky")," Dippé smiles, "which is the ability to take live action and project it onto a three-dimensional computer sculpture. You then take that three-dimensional sculpture and move it so the live action moves with it.

"With the three-dimensional model, you can line up the live action and cut it out," Dippé continues. "So if you take a picture of a guy who's walking through a set, you take the 3-D model of this guy and make it walk through the set-ups so they're registered together. Then you cut out the picture where the three-dimensional computer guy is and manipulate it."

Adding to the complexity of the scene is the fact that the T-1000 emerges from the wreckage in his shiny metallic form—which, mirrorlike, had to reflect his surroundings. To accomplish this, photographs of all the surroundings were taken on the set from the T-1000's point of view, then fed into the computer to build a three-dimensional arena for the character to reflect on his chrome body.

"The reflections were created by a relatively established computer graphics system called Cubic Reflection maps, where we go on the set, take photos and rebuild them in the computer," explains Williams. "So we photographed the front, back, left, right, top and bottom views, ending up with six different views. Then we constructed an invisible Cubic Reflection map, so essentially what we had was the character reflecting the environment in his chrome."

Various forms of the mksticky process were used throughout T2, including the scene where the T-1000 distorts his body while walking through a locked bar door in the mental hospital. Dippé notes there was "a lot of staging and editing to build up the drama and timing of that shot.

"First, we shot the live action of Robert Patrick pretending he was going through the bars," Dippé elaborates. "He took a half step, and then he kind of slowed down as if he was forcing himself through the bars, and then he sped up again as if he'd just gone through. Next, we shot the plate of the bars where they would have been if he'd been walking through them. On the computer, we match-modeled those bars and match-modeled Patrick's head, and then we projected the live-action Patrick onto the 3-D model of him in the computer. Using the computer, we had his head go through the computer bars, and where the computer bars were, they distorted his head as if it was mercury."

With all these state-of-the-art abilities, it's no wonder the T-800 finally meets his match in the T-1000. A simple Arnold punch might give any average person permanent brain damage, but the muscleman's bops to the T-1000's head hardly make a dent in this polyalloy being in their climactic fight for the future.

"First, we shot Schwarzenegger punching into thin air, as if he was hitting Patrick," explains Dippé. Next, a shot of Patrick jerking his head back as if somebody had hit him was filmed. The two images were eventually placed together, and using mksticky, "the hand disappears as if it's gone into the head. What we've done here is again match-modeled a chrome body to a live-action Robert Patrick, and we essentially wipe between the two."

Though the majority of ILM's major setpieces were designed particularly for T2, some software was redesigned and adapted from previous ILM projects. "You'll notice the similarity between when the T-1000 is swimming into the helicopter, forming into a man, and the pseudopod water snake from *The Abyss*," notes Williams. "We reused some of the same technology in that we scanned in faces in the snake in *The Abyss* using Cyberware."

A helicopter was suspended in midair via a crane in front of the actual building where this scene was being shot, in order to duplicate the same quality of lighting and reflection from the building. According to Dippé, if they had filmed the scene on a stage somewhere, they would have risked having scenes that didn't match.

"There was a camera in the helicopter, and we had Patrick push his head through the window," recalls Dippé, adding that once again, the actor's computer-generated model was superimposed over the live action, in order to manipulate the body into a liquid shape that flows into the chopper.

The reflection technique was of major importance here, so once again photographs were taken from every point of view of the seat where the T-1000 would eventually be regenerated via computer. "When you look at the polyalloy T-1000, all the reflected colors are coming from these photographs, which are accurate renditions of the set. So he looks like he's actually in there," notes Dippé.

Additionally, Cyberware scanned Patrick's head for the sequence where the T-1000 disguises himself as a checkerboard floor, eventually reforming back into a man, proving that this future warrior's camouflage techniques are state-of-the-art as well. "We had him pose in a rather neutral expression for that," remembers Dippé. "We digitized his head, and what we did with the computer was some blending by interpolating between the 3-D model of the head and a 3-D plate floor. It was kind of simple, but it was basically taking this flat floor and sort of turning it into an image of Patrick's head lying back on it."

THE T-1000'S HELICOPTER SCENE HAS A SPECIAL DISTINCTION: IT'S THE FIRST TIME A COMPUTER-GENERATED CHARACTER HAS "SPOKEN" IN A FILM.

Though Cameron wound up cutting a few dialogue scenes from the film, only a couple of minor FX moments were trimmed, including some ILM shots of the T-1000 malfunctioning after he has regrouped from being frozen by liquid nitrogen. "There was a really fantastic sequence where he starts to mimic anything he touches," says Dippé. This missing section has the T-1000 placing his hand on a yellow-and-black-striped OSHA railing and picking up the patterns on his hand. Aware of his technical malfunctioning, the T-1000 eventually shakes off the patterns.

"There was also a shot where you see him walking across a metal diamond plate floor, and the diamond plates are creeping up his leg," adds Dippé. "It was a real intense sequence, but it hurt the pacing of the film."

Though *T2* has opened up a whole new set of boundaries for digital filmmakers, both Williams and Dippé feel that it will never completely replace traditional film techniques, such as prosthetic work, stop-motion and go-motion. As with *T2*, however, they believe it will work together with those methods to create far more advanced and realistic-looking FX.

"What you're going to see is that we're going to be working a lot closer with people like Stan [Winston]," says Williams. "It will never replace craftsmanship; computers are secondary objects. They're a pencil. They need a hand to move them in a theoretical sense. In other words, they'll only perform as well as they are driven."

Already ILM has parlayed their current knowledge into a slate of other projects, including *Memoirs of an Invisible Man*, *Star Trek VI* and *Hook*. Still, although the technological future war may have been averted at the end of *T2*, a different kind of battle is up ahead for ILM: the one that helps them find the right film to allow them to take the next big leap in changing the face of moviemaking illusions.

"*T2* has allowed us to go to the next generation, and that's the basis of our current work," asserts Dippé. "We're one of the leaders in developing and inventing this whole filmmaking arena and vocabulary. We're turning film into clay, and can do anything we want to. People look at technology as scary, but you don't have to be afraid, because with the computer you can control anything. In truth, it's a freeing device. It's like adding more keys to a keyboard. It extends the instrument of filmmaking."

THIS EARLY SCENE HAD TO "SELL" THE OPTICAL FX TO THE AUDIENCE—AND IT MADE A BUYER OUT OF EVERYONE.

"TOTAL RECALL" MAGIC

ROB BOTTIN'S EYE-POPPING FX DISTINGUISHED *Total Recall* FROM OTHER GENRE FILMS.

BY BILL WARREN

The house is a quiet oasis in the Van Nuys/Sherman Oaks area of the San Fernando valley, hidden behind shrubbery and a high fence. Actor and occasional FX crewman Don (*The Howling*) McLeod lives here, but it's Rob Bottin who answers the door, tall, bearded and deep-voiced—"the original Wookiee," as Peter Weller calls him. And Bottin later grins ruefully, "I gotta sorta fess up to that," he admits. Bottin plays a quick, odd joke on his interviewer, who's sworn to secrecy (in print—ask me in person), and then we adjourn to a patio table for a talk about *Total Recall*.

Bottin gives very long answers to questions, sometimes acting embarrassed when he thinks he's been rambling. But what he doesn't seem to realize is that because of who he is, he's automatically interesting. He is, after all, *Rob Bottin*, one of the most talented men in the area of special makeup FX. Many movie people feel that in terms of conceiving an idea, Bottin may be the very best there is. Again and again in the three-hour chat, he says that what he wants is to (a) amaze the audience and (b) top himself—in that order.

He first heard of *Total Recall* several years ago. "Back when I was a whiz kid—now I'm just a whiz, if even that—I used to hear about this *Total Recall* thing," Bottin remembers. "It was intriguing to me because of how strange it was touted to be. That attracts me, just because I like weird things, I've tried to gravitate toward doing the *incredibly* strange. But originally, I passed on it, and I'm lucky I did, because if I hadn't done *The Thing*, which was offered to me at about the same time, I probably wouldn't have gotten asked to do *RoboCop* or *Total Recall* again."

Bottin is not inclined to talk about the specifics of his FX work, how this or that effect was actually done. In talking to him, you get the feeling that this is not secrecy, but just because his mind doesn't work that way. What's fascinating is how his mind *does* work. He's phenomenally intelligent, far more so than, one suspects, he thinks himself, although he does take an understandable pride in his accomplishments. He has a very rich vocabulary which he uses with no trace of self-consciousness. And he's a great mimic, doing quick, accurate impressions of Joe Dante ("I was the first guy to do Joe Dante," he claims), John Hora, Paul Verhoeven, Clint Eastwood, Arnold Schwarzenegger, Jon Davison and others.

The most fascinating thing about Bottin is how he tackles and solves an idea, and that's what the talk ends up dealing with. He and his crew did all the incredible mutant makeups in the film, including Benny's pterodactyl arm, and all the birth defect deformities, but as impressive as those are, one of the most astounding sequences in *Total Recall* involves Quaid (Schwarzenegger) being disguised as an old, fat lady.

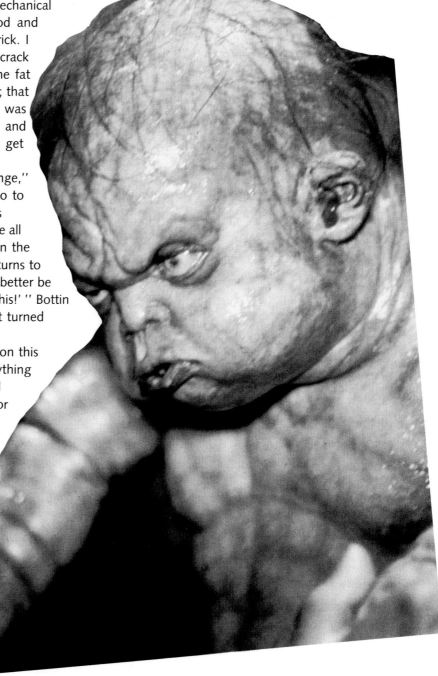

KUATO, THE MARTIAN REBEL LEADER CREATED BY BOTTIN AND CREW.

"All of the effects are so varied in this picture," Bottin says. "I'm not doing just a lot of transformations. I'm not doing just a lot of makeups. I'm not doing just a lot of mechanical effects. I'm not doing just a lot of blood and guts. I'm doing *all* of that. I did every trick. I don't mean I did it all myself; I have a crack crew of the best people in the world. The fat lady disguise is purely a mechanical effect; that effect actually happened while the crew was sitting there shooting it. It took months and months and months of trial and error to get that to work.

"Paul actually gave me the challenge," Bottin continues. "I showed up in Mexico to take some molds of Arnold; the film was already in progress at this time. There were all these extras on the set, just tons of them in the spaceport. Paul stops everything and he turns to me, and points a finger. 'This scene had better be good, because *you* talked me into all of this!' " Bottin exclaims, waving his arms. "Then he just turned around and went back to his work.

"So much emphasis was being put on this scene, but then, I put emphasis on everything I do, so I knew that I could deliver. But I knew it was going to be very difficult for everyone involved, at my studio.

"In the original script," Bottin goes on, "Arnold had boarded the spaceship, and put this case over his head; he pushed a button, steam shoots out, he pulls it off and he's another person. This threw me a little bit. Since my forte is coming up with these crazy things, obviously I'm looking to deliver as many possibilities to the audience as I can. I'm not picking on the writing. I don't want to make it sound like I didn't think it was wonderful from point one. But I was looking for a way to make it more visually striking, and I examined the thought that Arnold could put this thing on his head, and then pull it off, looking like another person. That's great, but it's too much like a dream. I can pretty much guarantee that there will never be one-second plastic surgery. So it didn't match the level of technology in the rest of the film, and also, if he can do this, why doesn't he do it throughout the film? Why doesn't he pull out his bag of tricks the moment the bad guys come by, and disguise himself again? Paul looks at me for a long time, and says [*in a slow, wondering tone*] 'You're right! So what do you think we should do?'

"I said, 'I have no idea! That's a tough nut to crack, conceptually.' So I go away. I'm thinking about it for a while, and decide that this is a disguise he can use only once. What if it malfunctions in the scene in which he needs to use it? I also thought that this is not a prosthetic, something that can be peeled off, because we've seen that so many times. Once again, I owe it to the audience to be fantastical. So, I thought, what if this thing is mechanical, not prosthetic? Maybe the voice starts slowing down and shorting out, maybe repeating itself.

"OK, so I thought, the mask is like that. If this fat lady is bigger than Arnold Schwarzenegger, that's one big lady. So this lady's head has got to be enormous, so there's room in there. This is a big, self-moving everything mask. I thought OK, OK, that's fun. I'm on to something here."

Bottin's delight as he retraces the steps his inventive mind took is infectious. It's almost like it's a machine he switches on that then runs on its own, finding its way to a novel, visually exciting conclusion.

On Mars, the old lady tells customs she will be there two weeks; when he asks if she brought fruits and vegetables, she says "Two weeks" again. Like a malfunctioning tape recorder, speeding up, his voice rising in pitch, Bottin cries, " 'Two weeks. Two

AN AMAZING SPLIT-LEVEL PROSTHETIC ALLOWS SCHWARZENEGGER TO PASS AS AN OLD WOMAN.

All *Total Recall* photos © Tristar

YOU NEVER KNOW WHO'S GOING TO TURN OUT TO BE A MUTANT WHEN BOTTIN IS ON THE CASE.

weeks two weeks twoweeks!' And she starts backing up. Richter [Michael Ironside, a villain, of course] and the others who're looking for Quaid turn and see, standing there like a sore thumb, this huge fat lady going 'Twoweeks!*twoweeks!TWOWEEKS!*' Richter knows it must be Quaid.

"Then the face—I thought, 'Here's where I really have to do some showmanship.' OK, it's mechanical, but flesh. So what the most amazing thing would be is if the flesh breaks down mechanically. The face peels open in horizontal sections like a Venetian blind. It splits apart and hangs there in the air, going *bwing-wingwing!* Arnold lifts it up, it closes, and he pulls it down to his chest."

Bottin described it this far to Verhoeven, who raised an interesting objection of his own. While all this is going on, the director asked, why don't Richter and his men just jump on Arnold and beat him up? Bottin, by now in love with his concept and aware that Verhoeven judges and dismisses weak ideas quickly, thought fast.

"I said, 'You know why they don't grab him?' He goes, 'Why! Why!' with a big grin on his face. And I say, 'Because, Paul, the head is also a *bomb*!' He starts laughing *his* head off, because Paul likes things like that." So in the movie, after his disguise shorts out and peels off, Quaid tosses the head to the nearest guard; it says "Get ready for a surprise!"—and explodes. All of this was contributed by Rob Bottin.

The artist is a private person. "I like to have my own space respected, which is why I'm reclusive. That's part of my policy with other people. I don't invade someone's privacy, even when casually talking to someone; that's bad manners." He's also cautious in dealing with a star like Schwarzenegger. "I don't want to mix my enjoyment of his work in his movies with talking to him as a professional."

Bottin suggested the next be set in italics and capital letters: *"I AM VERY IMPRESSED WITH JACK NICHOLSON'S ATTITUDE ON THIS."* When they worked on *The Witches of Eastwick*, "one of the things he said to me—and I'm not patting myself on the back, I'm just passing on to you what he really said—was, 'You're the best guy that does this kind of thing; I'm really good at doing my job, so let's just do it and have a good time.' I thought that was just great. When we got into a conversation, he asked *me* questions, and that sort of opened up the door between us."

Another effect in *Total Recall* that Bottin carefully thought his way through was JohnnyCab, the robot cabbie. "Paul was initially going to have no driver," Bottin says, but that disappointed the artist, since that had been done on *Knight Rider*. So Bottin had another idea. "If you were going to get into a cab that actually wasn't driven by a human being, you would get very nervous if you didn't see a driver. So they would probably have a generic man inside, like Johnny Cat kitty litter. JohnnyCab! This guy who's really happy and friendly and he's got a great big smile, he's very positive, his cab looks great and it's got checkers on it. He'll drive you anywhere, any time of night, doesn't sass you; he's a cab driver turned kind of chipper. He has repetitive dialogue, and you don't want to hear that when you want to get the hell out with bad guys chasing you."

Bottin had made a dummy of Weller for the first *RoboCop* that looked so real it fooled *Weller* (who was going nuts trying to figure out when he had done this scene before Bottin's videotape spilled the beans), and at first Bottin thought of doing a realistic robot cabbie. But Verhoeven pointed out that if Bottin made it *too* good, people would assume it was an actor, and what was the point of that? "So instead of making it look real, I had to make him look unreal. We actually put in glitches."

"I thought, whose face do I recall who has a big giant grin, and who really makes me laugh? No one else than Bob Picardo," who's turned up in several Bottin monster suits. Picardo was glad to pose for JohnnyCab, and after a tryout with Verhoeven, got the job of doing the voice as well. "He came up with JohnnyCab dialogue that had glitches in it!" exclaims Bottin happily. "Paul said that as far as the lips go, he didn't want them entirely in sync with the tape, so we tried to comedically come up with times when it isn't in sync."

At the beginning of the film, Arnold, on tape, tells a puzzled live Arnold to shove a gadget into his nose and pull out a brain implant that's serving as a tracking device for the bad guys. The production company sent over a small, pea-sized gadget to be pulled out. "I was disappointed," says Bottin, who contacted Verhoeven about this. "What we need," he told the director, "is something that will be awesome, and will possibly counteract the fact that what we are doing, in essence, is watching a man picking his nose. Whatever comes out of that nose should be sort of awesome in a very small way, because, obviously, Arnold is not going to pull a watermelon out of his nose. And just to add a little bit of fun, I have this thing come out of his nose, which is pretty awesome in itself, then I have it do a little transformation trick to get another little bit of fun from it." Again, an example of how Bottin, in charge of FX, comes up with ideas that make sense in terms of the film's *story*—and look sensational.

Throughout the conversation on this warm May afternoon, it's clear that Bottin thinks as much like a director as an FX expert, and he intends to move into directing, although he insists that, "I have always worked *for* the director, that big 'for.' I thought, *this* guy is telling the story and I am working *for* him. I would like to go on record thanking all the directors I have ever worked with for allowing me to *imagine* with them, in a big way. What a wonderful thing it was indeed that we could imagine, and we could do it, and make something be there. As a kid, we had to make our own go-carts, we had to make our own fun, but we didn't have the incredible amount of money you have in a movie to make fun. Now I'm a big kid and I get to make big fun."

EVEN WITH ALL OF VERHOEVEN'S TRADEMARK VIOLENCE, THIS WAS ONE OF THE MOST PAINFUL SCENES TO WATCH IN *Total Recall*.

PRICELESS

THE LATE VINCENT PRICE STARRED IN *Twice Told Tales*, AN ANTHOLOGY OF NATHANIEL HAWTHORNE'S STORIES.

BY TOM WEAVER

T he world's most cultivated horror star needs no introduction in these pages. Vincent Price was a living legend to fright film fans for most of the 50-plus years since he took the horror plunge with Universal's Tower of London in 1939. In the years since, he played a variety of roles in more than 100 films, made all over the world, but it was as a screen villain—cultivated but sinister—that Price made his most popular and acclaimed movies. In recognition of his preeminence in the horror field, Price—who passed away just before Halloween 1993 at the age of 82—was the very special guest of honor at the May 1990 FANGORIA Weekend of Horrors in Los Angeles where, following an introduction by director Roger Corman, the screen's foremost aristocrat of evil received ovation after ovation during an onstage interview with director Joe Dante. The questions were supplied by Dante, Tom Weaver and the audience.

FANGORIA: How did you become involved with Disney's short *Vincent*?
VINCENT PRICE: You know, if you're going to claim to be famous, you'd better be famous because Disney has made a movie named after you [*laughs*]. That is fame, let me tell you! Somebody from Disney sent me a storyboard for *Vincent*, and I thought it was such a wonderful idea—I loved the story. So I went over to meet [director] Tim Burton, and

Tim is kind of a mad fellow, a wonderful, mad little fellow. He had this marvelous idea and he showed me a little mockup of Vincent, the character, and then read me the script. And I said, "I will do it." So I went in and did the narration for him. It won a lot of prizes for Tim in little festivals all over the world. One of the reasons he did *Vincent* was that he was fascinated with, as he called it, "the Vincent Price persona"—how I

OPPOSITE PAGE TOP
PRICE (RIGHT)
DONNED ONE OF HIS
MOST FRIGHTENING
DISGUISES IN *Theater of Blood.*

OPPOSITE PAGE
BOTTOM
THE HORROR
LEGEND DELIVERED
HIS LAST SCREEN
TURN AS THE
INVENTOR OF
Edward Scissorhands.

was able to hide behind the evil. It's a wonderful film.

In Tim's *Edward Scissorhands*, I play the professor who creates Edward Scissorhands. Tim's a marvelous fellow, a really brilliant talent and a wonderful designer. He's sent me other things that he's made, and we've kept in touch.

FANG: When you made *House of Wax*, was that the point at which you had to decide whether you wanted to be a stage or movie star?

PRICE: Yes. I was offered a wonderful play in New York called *We're No Angels*, and it was a big, big hit, and every time I'd go by that theater in New York, I'd say, "Did I do the right thing?" But it eventually went off after a year, and *House of Wax* is *still* playing after 40 years! I don't know, really; you always wonder whether you've done the right thing or not. But I think I did because I loved *House of Wax*, it was great fun to make. And it was fun to be part of the growing motion picture technology.

FANG: The famous story about *House of Wax* is that the director, Andre de Toth, only had one eye—

PRICE:—and he couldn't see any of the 3-D effects! He'd go in and look at the film, and he'd ask, "What are all those people screaming about?" He never saw a *thing*!

FANG: One of your co-stars in that film was Charles Bronson.

PRICE: Yes—Charles Buchinski at the time. He was wonderful in it; he had no dialogue, but he was awfully good!

FANG: In preparing to do *House of Wax*, a remake of *Mystery of the Wax Museum*, did you look at Lionel Atwill's performance?

PRICE: No, that would have been a big, big mistake. I've never seen *Mystery of the Wax Museum*, unless I saw it as a kid—it came out when I was a youngster. I didn't see it—on purpose—because I didn't want to copy Atwill. And *House of Wax* was a different story.

While *House of Wax* was playing at the Paramount Theater in New

© 20th Century Fox

York—it played for about 30 weeks—I was doing a play there and I used to sneak into the back of the movie theater. And I'd have so much fun watching the people with those silly 3-D glasses on [laughs]. And they couldn't tell who *I* was, because I had glasses on, too! I'd always pick two teenage girls to sit behind, 'cause their reactions were marvelous. Finally at the end of one of the showings, these two girls were riveted and they were moving forward in their seats. And when I'm finally thrown into the vat of wax and I'm burned up and the steam comes up and it says "The End," I leaned forward and I said, "Did you *like* it?" Right up into orbit, they went!

FANG: You were directed by Alfred Hitchcock on his TV series.

PRICE: I was terribly excited about working with Hitchcock; he's one of the great moviemakers of all time. There were only two of us in it [Price and James Gregory], just two characters, and I thought it was going to be wonderful. It was a very elaborate thing called "The Perfect Crime," and I was really very thrilled to think of Hitchcock telling us what to do.

His entire direction was coming on the set one day and saying, "Faster." [*Laughs*] And so we did it a little faster and he said, "That's better. A little bit faster." Then he went over and slept [*laughs*]! I've read four books about Hitchcock recently, and he slept through *everything*—or gave the appearance of sleeping. He set things up so brilliantly that he didn't really have to watch very carefully.

FANG: *Angel Street* was one of your major successes on Broadway, and it was eventually made into the film *Gaslight* (1944). But you didn't end up playing the lead in the movie, Charles Boyer did.

PRICE: You never get a chance in the movies to play the same leading role that you've done on Broadway, or very seldom. But I did the play, and it ran for five years. It was an extraordinary story, a real theatrical story. The Schuberts [the theater owners] hated the play so much when they came to see a run-through that they refused to print the tickets for Monday. So the play opened on Friday, and on Saturday the reviews were raves, 100 percent. I've never read reviews like that in my life—"The best melodrama of all time" and so forth. And there were no tickets! The line outside the box office was there and the girls in the box office were writing the seat numbers down on slips of paper!

Finally Sunday came around. My wife was out on the West Coast, and I called her from New York and I said, "Isn't it wonderful?" There was a dead silence and then she said, "What do you mean, wonderful? It's the greatest tragedy of all time." I said, "The play is a hit! It's the biggest hit in town! What's this tragedy bit?" She said, "Pearl Harbor." I had read the papers, but I'd only read my own notices, I hadn't read about Pearl Harbor [*laughs*]. Isn't that a terrible story? Almost every show in New York closed right after that, except *Angel Street*, which ran five years.

FANG: You also wrote a play, too.

PRICE: How did you know that?

FANG: *Poet's Corner*. Were you happy with it?

PRICE: I loved it, I had a wonderful time. I was up in a famous summer theater called Skowhegan in Maine, and I showed it to the director there—I'd worked there before—and he said, "Well, it needs some work, but I like it and I'll do it—if you'll play in it." I said, "My God, *I* can't play in it—I'd be so nervous and self-conscious." He wound up putting me in a small part.

Well, I was a disaster, because every time somebody else would open their mouth and say one of my brilliant lines, I'd go [*Price gasps with awe*]. Or if it was a funny line [*Price bellylaughs*] —and I wasn't *meant* to laugh! Anyway, it was fun to do. I never tried another one, but it wasn't too bad.

FANG: You're one of the few actors who's played the Invisible Man twice, and when people see Invisible Man movies they often think, "How much work does this really involve?" For example, when you weren't there, did you come in those days?

PRICE: You come in. It's *endless!* There's a scene in *The Invisible Man Returns* where I take the clothes off a scarecrow, because I'm only invisible if I'm naked. (It's very cold!) I had to undress this scarecrow and put the clothes on myself, and it took nine hours. Today they have blue screens and chroma-key, but the way they did it in those days, the set was built and the camera anchored and they draped the whole set with black velvet. And then *I* was draped with black velvet. And whatever I put on myself, I put around the black velvet. But it took forever, because if you'd make the smallest mistake, you could be seen. It was very laborious and rather boring!

FANG: Is it true that the director of *The Invisible Man Returns* didn't speak English?

PRICE: Joe May spoke very, very little English. Thank God I spoke a little German—we could curse at each other. He was a great director in his day in Germany, but he really did have a bad time here because he didn't speak very much English at all.

I saw *The Invisible Man Returns* in a theater and there were two fellows in front of me, and at the end, when I returned to visibility, one of 'em said, "That'll teach you not to drink 10-cent whiskey!"

FANG: You gave wonderful comic performances in *Champagne for Caesar* and *His Kind of Woman.*

PRICE: I loved playing comedy, but I looked like a villain. And they were all villains, really, those comedic parts. But I love comedy, and it's much more difficult to play comedy than straight roles.

FANG: You were hilarious in *Tales of Terror*'s wine-tasting contest.

PRICE: [*Laughs*] That's a funny scene, I must say. They hired a fellow to come on the set and show us about wine-tasting, because people don't really taste wine, they *drink* it. So he was showing

THE ACTOR WAS A WELCOME PRESENCE IN THE LACKLUSTER *Dead Heat.*

us all these fancy things. All Peter [Lorre] and I did was just exaggerate them a tiny bit, and they were hysterical. I loved doing that.

FANG: Do you ever seek out and watch your old films?

PRICE: Every once in a while, if it was one that I enjoyed making. The ones with Roger Corman I loved, because we had such a good time making 'em. We worked hard, really hard—oh *boy*, he was a slavedriver! But it was wonderful fun, because he had it so carefully planned. He had Danny Haller doing the sets and Floyd Crosby on the camera; he got wonderful people around him and he just did a superb job. And, again, they were great fun.

FANG: When Ray Milland was asked how he liked working with Roger, he said, "I can't remember, because the pictures were made so quickly that I have hardly any memories of them."

PRICE: Roger did make pictures very quickly, but they were made thoroughly. They were brilliantly designed and brilliantly thought out. He was one of the best directors I ever worked with.

FANG: Which Corman film was the most satisfying?

PRICE: Well, I loved *The Masque of the Red Death*. We had one of the greatest cameramen in England [Nicolas Roeg], and we had a wonderful cast. And all the extras were from the Royal Ballet—but that you can only do in London, you can't do it here. You'd have to bring 'em out from New York! But it was a very exciting film, and I found it fun to work on.

FANG: Another fan favorite is *The Tomb of Ligeia*.

PRICE: *The Tomb of Ligeia* was the closest to Poe. Roger and I had often talked about the idea of doing a film in an actual location. We had this wonderful 12th-century abbey, and most of it was done right in there.

FANG: And *Pit and the Pendulum*?

PRICE: *Pit and the Pendulum* was one of Roger's triumphs, because that was a really difficult thing to bring off. You know, one of the problems with doing Edgar Allan Poe is that those are short stories, and you've got to make them into long films! And Poe doesn't take the trouble to explain why people are where they are, so you have to explain that. It was a difficult film to do, but I enjoyed it.

FANG: Were there any Poe stories that you would have liked to have done with Corman, but didn't?

PRICE: Yes. I would love to have done "The Gold-Bug" with Roger. "The Gold-Bug" was the first detective story—Poe was an extraordinary writer, and it would have been fun to do that "version" of him. Because many people don't realize that something like 65 percent of Poe's work is satirical—it isn't heavy, it isn't horror, it's satirical work. I did a television show one time called *An Evening with Edgar Allan Poe*, and in it I narrated a Poe story called "The Sphinx." It's about a man who thinks that he sees a monster, and it turns out to be a little moth.

FANG: Tell us about *Dragonwyck*.

PRICE: *Dragonwyck* was one of the best pictures I ever made. It was Joe Mankiewicz's first picture [as director] and it was the fourth picture that I'd done with Gene Tierney: I also did *Laura* [1944] with her, and that's really one of the best pictures ever made. It's not a pretentious picture; it was perfect—the best thing that Otto Preminger ever did.

FANG: Your "typing" in the late '50s as a horror star began with your association with William Castle. He brought a sense of fun to going to the movies, a kind of showmanship sadly missing today.

PRICE: He was a great showman. There was a wonderful article in one of the airplane magazines not too long ago about "What Happened to Show Biz?" and it brought up Bill Castle and the things that he did. The crazy things, like *The Tingler*. But he was wonderful! I mean, who would ever do a black and white movie and have one scene in

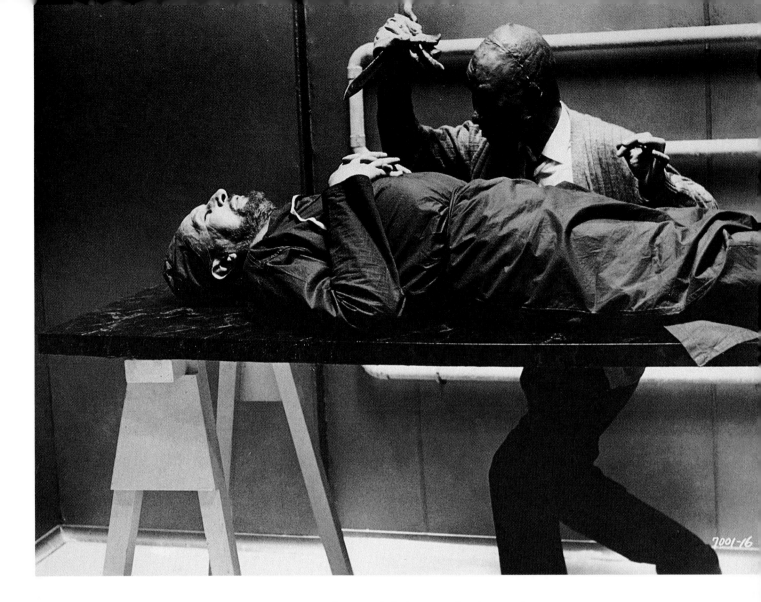

color, where the lady turns on the water in the bathtub and it's *bloo-oo-ood!*

FANG: When Castle would come to you with a script, would he already have the gimmick in mind?

PRICE: Yes, I think so. Like *House on Haunted Hill*, with the emerging skeleton! When he was looking for a haunted house, he went out and found a great Frank Lloyd Wright house—one of the most modern pieces of architecture in the world—and he used *that* as the haunted house! And there's nothing like that first scene, where all the guests that I've invited arrive by hearse! He was a nutty fellow, but great fun and very inventive.

The opening night of *House on Haunted Hill*, I was in a little theater in Baltimore. In the movie I reel this skeleton in using a winch, and then there'd

be a real skeleton in the theater that would shoot down over the audience. Well, I was in this theater with a great many young people in it—and they panicked! They knocked all the seats out of the theater [*laughs*]! They just took down the first five rows. I *loved* it!

FANG: Could you tell us a little about Peter Lorre?

PRICE: [*Holding his nose and imitating Lorre*] Peter? [*Laughs*] The greatest imitation I ever heard of Peter Lorre in my life was by Peter Lorre. He held his nose and he talked like that, and that sounded just *exactly like* Peter Lorre [*laughs*]! At his funeral I read the obituary address for him, because all of his friends were dead—Humphrey Bogart and all of them were gone, and I guess I knew him as well as anyone at that time. He called himself a "face maker,"

BEHIND THE SCENES, PRICE POSED FOR THIS GAG SHOT IN *Scream and Scream Again.*

and he always denigrated actors. He played 'em down, said we're face makers and nothing else, we really don't have a brain in our heads. But he was a wonderful actor.

He also loved to rewrite the script. One time, in one of Roger's films, there was a scene where all Peter and I were doing was getting from one place to another, and there was some exposition there. I always know my lines and I was saying them, and Peter was sort of vaguely saying something else. I don't know what it was. And I said, "Oh, for Christ's sake, Peter, say the lines!" [*Laughs*] He said, "You mean that, old boy? You don't like *my* lines better?" I said [*sharply*], "No!" So he said all the lines—he knew every line in the script! But he didn't *like* to say them [*laughs*]!

FANG: Boris Karloff found Lorre a little off-putting, because he would not stick to the script.

PRICE: Yes, it was very annoying, it really was. Because no actor is funnier than a good writer.

FANG: Basil Rathbone?

PRICE: Basil—I sound like Pollyanna, don't I?—he was one of the nicest men that ever lived [*laughs*]! I did *Tower of London* with him; he was Richard III and he was absolutely marvelous in it. And he did a wonderful thing to keep everybody's spirits up—it was a rather heavy play and there were too many stars in it. He got us all together, all the cast—being the star, he could do this—and he said, "Let's make an agreement amongst ourselves. Let's never tell a dirty joke that we didn't hear after we were 14." Well, we'd all go home at night and think of all the dirty jokes that we'd heard *before* we were 14. And they were very funny [*laughs*]! They weren't particularly dirty, but they were very funny, and we'd come on the set the next day and tell these stories! Basil was a sweet man—a great prankster and joker, but a wonderful actor.

FANG: What were some of your most difficult films to make?

PRICE: I did a couple in Italy, which shall be nameless—

FANG: *Nefertiti*?

PRICE: *Nefertiti, Queen of the Nile* [1961]! God Almighty! And another one with Ricardo Montalban called *Gordon, Il Pirato Nero* [1962]—*Gordon, the Black Pirate*. I said, "Why *Gordon*?" [*Laughs*] Gordon, what kind of terrible name is that? Well, Gordon, I finally found out, was because of Byron, who was Lord Gordon—he had lived in Italy. On *Gordon* they lost the soundtrack, so we dubbed it. But we had so many different nationalities in it that we had to hire lip readers in everything but *Watusi* [*laughs*]—it was impossible! I don't think anybody ever saw it.

FANG: What was it like making *The Last Man on Earth* in Rome?

PRICE: The problem doing *The Last Man on Earth* was that it was supposed to be set in Los Angeles, and if there's a city in the world that *doesn't* look like Los Angeles, it's Rome [*laughs*]. We would get up and drive out at 5:00 a.m., to beat the police, and try to find something that didn't look like Rome. Rome has flat trees, ancient buildings— we had a terrible time! And I was never so cold in my life as I was on that picture. I used to tip my driver a big sum to keep the car running, so I could change my clothes in the back seat.

FANG: *Conqueror Worm* reportedly was a very troubled film; your conflict with the director stemmed from the fact that he had originally wanted someone else for the part—

PRICE: —and *told* me so [*laughs*]! When I went on location to meet him [Michael Reeves] for the first time, he said, "I didn't want you and I still don't want you, but I'm stuck with you!" That's the way to gain confidence! He had no idea how to talk to actors. He came up to me one day [after a take] and he said, "Don't shake your head!" I said, "What do you mean? I'm not shaking my head." He said, "You're shaking your head! Just don't shake your head." Well, that made me so self-conscious that I was poker-faced—and, as it turned out, he was right! He wanted it that concentrated, so it would be that much more menacing. He could have been a wonderful director. . . such a sad, sad death. . .

FANG: How about *The Abominable Dr. Phibes*?

PRICE: *Abominable Dr. Phibes*, and *Dr. Phibes Rises Again*, are really funny pictures, two of the funniest pictures ever made. Scary, but funny—each one of the murders has a little fillip to it that makes it funny. The guy who directed them [Robert Fuest] was a madman—and wonderful. He would say, "Do this," and you *did* it, because there was nothing else to do! It was so mad and so crazy but they were great fun to do. I loved doing those two.

FANG: How did you get involved with Alice Cooper on his *Welcome to My Nightmare* album?

PRICE: I did a show for a long time called *The Hollywood Squares*, and on *Hollywood Squares* you met everybody [*laughs*]—everybody in the world! It was great fun because the comics were all on it, and I love comics. Alice and I became friends, and he asked me if I would do this thing. Just like Michael Jackson asked me to do *Thriller*—which is still the biggest-selling album in the history of the medium. If you're going to do those raps—I notice that I am now sort of the grandfather of the raps, or the great-grandfather [*laughs*]—they'd better be good. And *Thriller* was a wonderful rap, really marvelous.

FANG: Tell us about working with Diana Rigg in *Theater of Blood*.

PRICE: Diana Rigg—she's a killer, that girl, one of the most sexy and attractive ladies I've ever met in my life. She took over my spot in *Mystery!* as the host; I'd done it for eight years and I thought that was enough of that, and so she's

AUDIENCES FIRST GOT A LOOK AT THE NEW SCREAM STAR IN *The Invisible Man Returns.*

PICTURES Present
ELLS' Fantastic
THIS WORLD
Show

The INVISIBLE MAN RETURNS

R CEDRIC HARDWICKE VINCENT PRICE · NAN GREY

come in and is doing it now. She's awfully good, a wonderful actress.

FANG: You've worked a number of times with your fellow Geminis Peter Cushing and Christopher Lee, and you're very close to them.

PRICE: Christopher, when you first meet him—if you don't get along right away, he's a rather pompous man [*laughs*]. He's very British and terribly proper. For some reason or other we got along wonderfully, and we're like two girls—we get on the telephone together and crack jokes. We save up jokes and gossip and all kinds of things! I don't think he does that with anybody else— we just have the best time together, and I'm devoted to him. Peter Cushing is a very proper man, a very sad man—he lost his wife years ago, and he's never gotten over it. But we're all born within a day of each other—not in the same year, as they hasten to point out [*laughs*]!

FANG: What was it like to work on the old *Batman* series?

PRICE: Egghead? I've run into a large amount of criticism over the years; people would say, "Why did you do such a crappy thing as *Batman*?" Well, *Batman* wasn't crappy, it was one of the funniest shows ever on the air, really hysterical. They were broad, they were farcical, but they were wonderful. I must get a hundred pictures of Egghead a week to sign—*Batman* is all over the world now, they replay it in England, in Germany, everywhere. I'm so sick of that picture of me holding the egg! [*Laughs*]

FANG: What did you think of the new version of *The Fly?*

PRICE: When the new *Fly* came out, I thought they were going to call it *The Zipper* [*laughs*]. Anyway, when it came out, I got a lovely letter from Jeff Goldblum saying, "I loved your *Fly*, hope you like mine." [*Laughs*] That was very sweet, it was an adorable letter. And he loved the original *Fly*. So I went to see his, and I thought parts of it were marvelous, up until the end. Then he didn't

turn into a fly, he turned into a *glob*. There was nothing left of him. They went too far and lost credibility.

Horror films must be logical. You must be able to believe some part of them—not all of it, but you must be able to believe that this *could* happen. Otherwise it's not frightening.

FANG: Being that you're the true master of classic horror, what is the attraction for you for horror and terror?

PRICE: *You.* People enjoy it. And when they're made with the imagination that Roger Corman put into 'em, and that the other people I've worked with put into 'em, people love 'em. They're like fairy tales—they have a quality of the unreal and yet they're real. They scare you and you scream and then you laugh at yourself. They're great fun.

FANG: There are no derogatory stories about you.

PRICE: There are very few, because I like people. And I think that if you like people, you get along with people and they don't dislike you. I know of so many people who are miserable in this business—really miserable—and I never could understand it, because they're so bloody lucky to be in and to stay in it. I really think it's a wonderful business and people should be very grateful for being part of it.

FANG: A thousand years from now, if there was only one Vincent Price movie left, which one should it be?

PRICE: *Dragonwyck. Dragonwyck* was a very difficult part to play, because he's a crazy man, a monomanic, and yet didn't know it. So it was a challenge. I think *Dragonwyck*'s a very good film.

ROBERT ENGLUND: FREDDY LIVES!

BY MARC SHAPIRO

This is what we call the hero glove," says Robert Englund as he flexes his hand inside Freddy Krueger's best-known prop. "It's our equivalent of the Magnum Clint Eastwood uses in the *Dirty Harry* movies."

Englund clicks the razor fingers together a couple of times, producing a rusty-sounding scratch that is picked up by the microphone attached to his shirt collar. "How's that?" he asks.

"That's fine," says the interviewer standing behind an *E! Entertainment* camera. Englund unhooks the mike, does some minor gladhanding with the crew and producer and wanders over to where *Entertainment Tonight* is setting up shop.

"OK," laughs Englund as he settles into a chair. "Who's next?"

For Englund, this is a rare day off in the grueling production schedule of *Freddy's Dead: The Final Nightmare*. It's a chance to stroll with his wife and dog at the outdoor location where Roseanne Barr and Tom Arnold are shooting their cameo. It's also his time to run the television celebrity magazine gauntlet and assure people in TV-land that his latest film is indeed *The Final Nightmare*, at least as far as he believes. (Since this interview was conducted, however, plans have been announced for a seventh film, starring Englund and written and directed by *Nightmare* creator Wes Craven.)

Englund admits to having mixed emotions regarding his *Final Nightmare* outing. He knew it was coming, and greased the wheels of a career beyond Freddy by appearing as a different kind of heavy in the unsuccessful Andrew Dice Clay film *The Adventures of Ford Fairlane*. But now that the end appears to be at hand, the actor is looking forward to exploring different kinds of roles.

ROBERT ENGLUND TURNED FREDDY KRUEGER INTO THE '80'S MOST RECOGNIZABLE HORROR VILLAIN.

"Freddy's been real good to me, and I'm going to miss playing him," Englund confirms. "But to a certain extent, I'm also tired of playing Freddy and am ready to move on. I don't think I should do another horror character over and over again. Otherwise, I'm open to whatever comes my way."

The actor is candid as he describes the price that playing Krueger has ultimately exacted on his profession. "I've had to turn down another whole career's worth of work because of Freddy," he reveals. "That's one of the main reasons I'll be glad to see Freddy go. Certain seasons are better for making movies than others and, unfortunately, the periods when we made the *Nightmare* movies were also the times when a lot of other films were being made. I was basically trapped by time.

"I missed a directing gig in France two years ago because of *Nightmare 4*," he continues. "I would have loved to have tested myself that way. At one point, the *Freddy's Dead* start time was pushed back and I was offered the role of a KGB agent opposite one of my favorite actors, Rip Torn. But then they changed the schedule again, and I wasn't able to do it. Those were the kinds of missed opportunities I used to kick myself in the butt over. It was frustrating."

Four months later, *Freddy's Dead* is long completed, and Englund has wasted little time in getting a non-Freddy career going. The actor had returned from Leningrad, where he starred as demented, disfigured choreographer Anthony Wagner in the thriller *Dance Macabre*. Formerly titled *Terror of Manhattan* and originally intended as a follow-up to Englund's *Phantom of the Opera*, the film finds Englund portraying two characters; the main plot involves Wagner tutoring and becoming obsessed with a young American dancer, resulting in a series of bizarre murders.

THE ACTOR MADE A FEW NEW FRIENDS WHEN HE HOSTED THE *Horror Hall of Fame* TV SPECIAL.

All Freddy Krueger photos © New Line

"I get to do a lot of my best Anthony Perkins twitching in this film," chuckles Englund. "I'm really damaged goods. I won't blow the surprise by telling you the mystery role I play, but I liked the other part because it allowed me to be neurotic without wearing makeup.

"This movie is kind of a slasher-level version of *Ten Little Indians*," he continues. "It's more of a thriller than a horror film. There's a little bit of *Phantom of the Opera* in the storyline, but not in the character."

According to Englund, shooting *Dance Macabre* was an adventure, much of which involved working with a largely Russian production team. "The crew was very talented, but they work very differently," he observes. "When they move to a new location, that means there's no more working that day. Whenever a character dies in the film, the crew has to drink shots of vodka. They are very superstitious people. They're also not used to working long hours, and they probably never worked as hard as we worked them."

Under the direction of Greydon (*Without Warning*) Clark, Englund toiled on *Dance Macabre* shortly after shooting the pilot for Wes Craven's NBC television series *Nightmare Cafe*. The ill-fated show featured Englund, Jack Coleman and Lindsay (*Dead Heat*) Frost as the ghostly denizens of an eatery where the futures of customers at the crossroads of heaven and hell are decided. Englund calls it a cross between *The Twilight Zone* and *The Devil and Daniel Webster*, with a little bit of *Angel Heart* and *Topper* thrown in.

"It's a weird mixture," he remarks, adding that Craven, Jack Sholder and Philip (*Dead Calm*) Noyce are among the genre pros to helm episodes. "It's definitely a show that needs careful handling to succeed."

Blackie, Englund's continuing character in the anthology, is a spooky fallen angel and a bit of a cynic. "I'm there to manage this purgatory and bet that people who come through the restaurant are all going to go to hell," he explains. "I'm also constantly seeing elements in people that remind me of my own humanity. *Nightmare Cafe* plays with time and reality, making things interesting."

The role is a change of pace from his part in *Ford Fairlane*, which was less intellectual and more physically taxing. "I had little but fight scenes in that film, but that's nothing new," Englund shrugs. "I've been beat up by some of the biggest names in the industry over the years. I had a stunt double on the movie, but we didn't use him much and, in at least one scene, I wish we had. I was doing some kickboxing and ended up tearing a hernia, which required surgery and knocked me out for most of the summer."

Englund is now actively seeking financing for a script called *Wicked Flesh*, which promises to put a new twist on a genre staple. "It's kind of a sexual vampire thing," he describes. "The bloodsucker movie is hot right now, so why not a vampire that sucks hormones?" In addition, he is using his time to wade through the scripts that have started to come his way.

"I have so many friends who are doing horror films that I'd love to just go do cameos and become the new Dick Miller," Englund claims. "The only problem is that when these films are sold overseas, I would have no control about how my name would be exploited. Something like that could hurt my economic integrity if I do a film for a Dario Argento or a Clive Barker."

After more than a decade on the big screen, the actor also expresses a desire to return to one of his best-known TV characters. "I'd love to do Willie again," reveals Englund when the prospect of a rumored "V" revival comes up. "I'd work with [series producer] Ken Johnson anytime. If it were to happen, we could work things out.

"I'm serious about getting back into television," he continues. "I'd love to do a

© 20th Century Fox

sitcom. I could show up on Monday, eat a bagel, drink some coffee and leave at 2:00 in the afternoon. Television is really good exercise for an actor, and it would instantly remind people of the other kind of work I do.''

Before the job rush hit, Englund was planning on a leisurely post-Freddy life. ''I want to be able to go to a couple of Fango conventions, pick up a couple of 'V' lunch boxes, talk to fans and basically let them know that while Freddy is dead, Robert is still around. I'm on a mission of sorts: to let people know that I'm going to be up to other things. But I don't really worry about the audience losing interest in me once Freddy's gone. Even during the *Nightmare* years, I would get letters from fans that indicated they were very knowledgeable about my career before *A Nightmare on Elm Street.* So I have no fears that people will forget about me.''

However, Englund is aware that Freddy will never really go away. The first five films are enjoying a healthy video and cable afterlife. The two seasons of *Freddy's Nightmares* are hitting tape and are primed for worldwide syndication. And while he concedes that the *Nightmare* films' popularity in the U.S. has reached its limit, Freddy is still going great guns in the rest of the world.

And so, while Englund insists he is ''looking forward to putting some distance between myself and the whole Freddy thing,'' he is philosophical in attempting to put the phenomenon in perspective. ''I'm anxious to have the time to go back and get some hindsight on what it all meant,'' he affirms. ''What these films have meant to horror is obvious. They've opened the doors to what can be done in the genre. I'm convinced that if there had not been *Nightmare* films, you would not have had many of the other horror movies being made.

''A whole lot of talented filmmakers have gotten together, worked from what Wes Craven created and turned it into a wonderful series of films,'' he continues. ''Some have been better than others but, even at their worst, they have been better than most recent horror films. It's a wonderful legacy of filmmaking to look back on. It's a series of movies that people will go back to in the years to come and will hold up as something special that went on in the '80s. These movies are a part of film history. But this is the time to let it go,'' Englund concludes, ''and go on to something else.''

**TOP LEFT
DESPITE** *Freddy's Dead,* **ANOTHER** *Nightmare* **WAS SOON ON THE WAY FROM ORIGINAL CREATOR WES CRAVEN.**

**TOP RIGHT
EVEN AT HIS CRAZIEST, ENGLUND WAS NO MATCH FOR ANDREW DICE CLAY AND A FEW TAXING FIGHT SCENES IN** *Ford Fairlane.*

"HALLOWEEN" AND THE SHAPES OF WRATH

BY MARC SHAPIRO

STALKING HIS WAY
THROUGH FOUR
Halloweens, MICHAEL
MYERS BECAME THE
SCREEN'S SCARIEST
BOGEYMAN.

Michael Myers is not the easiest killer to play. He does not have the winning personality (unless you count the ghoulish non-face he presents to the world) or the way with words of a Freddy Krueger. He's not as light on his feet as Jason. And he's certainly not a picture of sartorial splendor like Leatherface.

Michael Myers, pure and simple, is a blue-collar kind of guy, a nine-to-five, lunchbox-toting horror hardhat who believes in administering an honest day's grue for an honest day's pay. He's stalk 'n' slash's man of a single face and no words.

Just who plays this guy with the one-slash mind? People on the way up? People on the way down? People on their way to selling real estate? Winos who need $1.98 for a jug of Night Train Express?

The guys who don the Myers mask are a pretty solid bunch of working stiffs. To a man, they're still in the movie business (and that includes Tommy Lee Wallace and the handful of obscuros who have played the Shape in second-unit cameos) and take their celebrity with a grain of salt.

The roll call begins. These are the guys who have essayed this most difficult of roles in *Halloween*, *Halloween II*, *Halloween 4* and, most recently, *Halloween 5*. So cozy up to the fire and listen to their memories of the night their alter ego came home.

Michael 1: The Perfect Puppet

Nick Castle is currently a hotshot multicredited director, noted for *Dennis the Menace*, *Tap*, *The Boy Who Could Fly* and *The Last Starfighter*, but it wasn't always that way. Before he went mainstream, a fellow named Michael Myers entered his life.

"John Carpenter and I had gone to film school together and had become real close friends," recalls Castle. "I was in the process of putting my first film together and learning the filmmaking ropes. John had already done a couple of films and was getting ready to start *Halloween*, so I asked him if I could hang out on the set and take in what he was doing. John said, 'Since you're going to be hanging around anyway, why don't you play the killer?'

"The idea of a low-budget horror movie sounded like fun," continues Castle, "but I was thinking to myself, 'Why does he want *me* to play this killer?' John said it was because he liked the way I walked."

Being the first in what would become a long line of maniacs didn't offer Castle a deep well of history to consult for the part. Background had nothing to do with playing the infamous Shape.

"There was no inspiration involved at all," chuckles Castle. "I know I sure didn't get a whole lot of ideas from the director. I would go up to John and say, 'How should I play this?' and he would say, 'Just walk.' The mask itself was doing more acting than I was. Playing Michael was more or less a situation where I would pop in and out of scenes, and John would tell me to do this or do that. He pretty much puppeteered me through the whole film."

The biggest piece of acting Castle did in *Halloween* comes at the beginning of the film, in the sequence where an unmasked Michael jumps on a car during an early morning rain-drenched scene. "It was 4:00 a.m., and it was real cold. Here they were, drenching me with water," he winces. "By that film's standards, that was a major bit of acting for me. Most of the time, I was just another John Carpenter tool, just a bit of furniture."

CREATIVE KILLING BECAME ALL THE RAGE IN THE SLASHER SUBGENRE, BUT MICHAEL TENDED TO STICK TO HIS MOST TRUSTWORTHY WEAPON.

The walking couch did manage some minor bits of subtlety that, in the telling, will probably have you running out to rent the video. "The scenes in which I carried the women around were a real challenge," chronicles the actor/director. "I had to do it in a casual manner so it wouldn't look like I was struggling, which I really was. In the scene where I stab that guy in the kitchen, John suggested that I add that little cock of my head so that it would look as if Michael was an artist admiring his work. I tried to add little notions every once in a while, but with a character like Michael Myers, there really is not a whole lot you can do. I was kind of like the plant in *Little Shop of Horrors*."

Castle recalls little socializing with Donald Pleasence on the *Halloween* set. "We had very few scenes together, and when he wasn't on the set, he was elsewhere," Castle recounts. "I did hang out with Jamie Lee Curtis and found her to be a delightful person with a great sense of humor.

"It was a fun film to do, and I was learning a lot about filmmaking by just being on the set. *Halloween* ended up putting the whole directing experience in a more realistic perspective for me."

This enlightenment carried over to his reaction the first time he saw *Halloween* in a theater with paying customers. "It confirmed my suspicions that *Halloween* would turn out as a well-done movie," he assesses. "I knew when Michael was going to be popping out, so I wasn't particularly afraid of anything, but I was amazed to discover people actually being scared by the film."

While Nick Castle went on to co-script *Escape from New York* with Carpenter and to pursue other directing and writing chores, he did keep track of the *Halloween* series. "I had no idea *Halloween* would go on to become what it has become," he says. "I felt John had done a very good one-shot film, and that would be it. I really didn't think that *Halloween II* was as successful. It wasn't as scary, and my image of Michael Myers as a long and lean character played more to the tone of the films than the chunky actor who played him in *Halloween II*."

Despite his interest in the second installment, Castle had no

**THE SHAPE STRIKES
A FAMILIAR POSE IN**
Halloween 5.

desire to repeat his Michael Myers role. Nor was he interested in parlaying his success into another slasher character. "No, nobody came up to me after that film and asked me to play Jason or Leatherface," laughs Castle. "I think they realized that all I amounted to was the manipulation of the director and the cameraman. They knew I was just the guy under the mask."

Michael 2: Scare a Secretary

Dick Warlock did not start out with the idea that he'd play Michael Myers in *Halloween II*. But hey, this is Hollywood, land of opportunity!

"I was applying for the job of stunt coordinator on *Halloween II*," remembers the veteran stuntman, whose genre credits include *The Thing* and *The Abyss*. "One day I was taking a meeting with director Rick Rosenthal, and I spotted the Michael Myers mask sitting on a table in a room. Just for a laugh I put the mask on, walked down a hall, growled a little and just about scared a secretary to death. Then I thought, 'Hey, if I'm this good, maybe I ought to try out for the part.' So I tried out and got it."

Soon the prop department gave Warlock a Michael Myers element that God had neglected to issue the stuntman at birth. "I'm only 5-foot-9," explains Warlock, "and Michael has always been pictured as this big 6-footer or better. So they outfitted me with lifts in my boots to get the extra height."

Warlock entered *Halloween II* wearing two hats, that of stunt coordinator and main Shape, and he remembers having to adjust his thinking accordingly. "One minute I was menacing everybody, and the next I was thinking like a stunt coordinator, trying to be careful of the people I was working with," Warlock explains.

Two sequences in particular required Warlock to do a juggling act to keep everyone happy, not to mention alive. "You remember that scene where I dunk the girl in the jacuzzi full of boiling water? Well, we worked out a real subtle series of signals with the actress so, if she needed air or was feeling panicky underwater, she could let me know," he says. "The final death scene, where Michael and Loomis burn, was a tricky one. There was a lot of preparation for that scene, and then the fire did not turn out like the director wanted, so we had to shoot it again. Mentally, I wasn't playing the character of Michael at that point."

Still, he does recall undergoing a definite Michaelish personality change when the mask was firmly in place. "It wasn't something that I felt so much as it was in the vibes I gave off to others," he says. "My wife began to sense a real bizarre feeling when she was around me during the making of that movie. I couldn't put a finger on it, but it was something that people who knew me saw and felt."

Warlock describes the kills in *Halloween II* as fairly standard. "The needle in the girl's temple and the hammer in the guard's skull were done with dummy heads," he reveals. "Rick Rosenthal was good on the effects scenes. He never pushed the scenes or the actors to the point where there was a chance of anybody getting hurt."

Still, Warlock recalls that, creatively, something was hurting on the *Halloween II* set—a growing difference of opinion between Rosenthal and co-writer/producer Carpenter. "There was definitely a personality conflict between Rick and John," admits Warlock. "Some of the crew had complained privately that Rick had made some mistakes and that John was only attempting to save the film. If there was a controversy, I would say it was a relatively minor one. What did happen is that John came in at one point and shot three days of second-unit work. One of the scenes John shot was the sequence where the little boy playing in the cowboy hat bumps right into Michael. What most people don't know is that the little boy was my youngest son."

Warlock goes on to detail another *Halloween II* sequence that literally allowed

THERE'S NO
OBSTACLE THAT
Halloween's **VILLAIN**
CAN'T BREAK
THROUGH.

the stuntman to play two characters in the same scene. "It was at the beginning of the film, when the phony Shape walks away and is hit by a police car. I drove the police car and another stuntman played Michael in that one scene. I don't remember why the scene was shot that way, but I ended up getting two credits in the film because of it," he chuckles.

Warlock is not a real horror fan, but he has seen and worked in enough of them to know what makes them work, so it should come as no surprise that the problem he sensed while filming *Halloween II* was confirmed when he saw the completed film.

"The anticipation of seeing things is what makes movies like *Halloween* work," decides Warlock, "and from the moment the film began, I knew the audience was seeing too much of Michael. I felt if you had seen a bit less of the Shape, the film would have worked a lot better.

"But I had a real good time playing Michael," he continues, "so much so that I was disappointed when they hired George Wilbur to play him in *Halloween 4*. I would *love* to play Michael Myers again."

But the end of *Halloween II* did not end Warlock's ties to the series. The stuntman went on to do a bit in the Shapeless *Halloween III: Season of the Witch*. Later, while out on location for Mark Lester's *Firestarter*, he discovered first-hand the long memories *Halloween* fans have. "I was sitting in my trailer," recalls Warlock, "when all of a sudden there was this knock on the door. These two local kids happened to be wandering by the set, spotted my name on the trailer and immediately recognized it as the guy who played Michael in *Halloween II*.

"These kids were so excited that they insisted I come over to their house, meet their parents and watch videos. Now, I know that wasn't the first night Michael Myers came home," laughs Warlock, "but I'll bet it was the first time he's ever been invited."

Michael 3: Babe in the Woods

George Wilbur's memories of Michael are fairly fresh at the time of this interview, but the mild-mannered stuntman's tour of duty in *Halloween 4* (subtitled *The Return of Michael Myers*) has already started to pay celebrity dividends. "I signed some autographs," explains Wilbur, whose career contains such genre highlights as *Blacula*, *Planet of the Apes* and *Poltergeist.* "My daughter was all excited and kept telling me how famous I'm going to be."

Wilbur comes across as too nice to commit the round of killings he had to perform in *Halloween 4*, and it was an out-of-character stint that had him more than a little bit concerned. "Playing Michael was an *acting* role, a matter of creating an illusion," he says. "Michael hasn't gotten into my personality, but looking back on all the evil things I did in that film, I was worried what my friends and family would think when they saw it."

Wilbur landed the coveted Shape assignment because "I was big and coordinated," he claims. "Michael gets hit, shot, rolls off a truck and falls down a well, so they needed to have somebody who could do a lot of different things."

Specifically, that meant doing things *to* people. Once you get past the head-bashing, neck-ripping and shotgun-impaling, there was the constant menace of Michael directed toward Jamie, who was played by young actress Danielle Harris.

"I took particular care when I was working with the little girl," explains Wilbur. "With all the scenes where I'm chasing her and terrorizing her, I was real concerned about whether she was going to bed with Michael Myers on her mind. So I would always laugh and joke with her before any heavy scenes, to let her know that it was only me and that what we were doing was only make-believe. I made sure she knew that I was not going to hurt her."

In a bit of self-examination, Wilbur concedes that he enjoyed his stalker shtick. "I got a big kick out of being this mean guy," he confesses. "The things we did in *Halloween 4* were so over the top and extreme that they were actually fun to do. I mean, Michael doesn't just get hit by a truck once but *three times* in the same scene, and he just keeps coming back for more. The character is not just killing people, he's ripping them to pieces. Playing somebody so indestructible and unstoppable was a challenge."

Having fun did not get in the way of Wilbur's looking to his stunt side when a scene called for Michael to menace two stunt doubles on a rooftop. "There's a certain amount of danger built into any high-fall stunt," explains Wilbur, "so I was out there real early, positioning myself and checking cables with the stunt coordinator. I made sure I would not end up missing a cue and forcing the stunt to be repeated. I really did not want to mess it up."

While Wilbur did not botch his drop, a miscalculation on just how gory *Halloween 4* should be resulted in his returning to the crime scene a few weeks after completion for an additional day of shooting that added some blood and guts to the film. "I was surprised when they called me back," says Wilbur. "I thought I was finished with Michael, but it was another day's work and I sure enjoyed the paycheck."

Though he didn't don the mask for *Halloween 5*, Wilbur wouldn't mind re-enlisting for a future sequel stint. "If I play Michael again, I think my reaction to the job will be the same as it was this time," he reasons. "I'll put on the mask, look in a mirror and see Michael Myers."

LEFT
WHO NEEDS
ELABORATE
MAKEUP?

THIS GIRL WAS ONE
OF THE FEW WHO
WERE SURPRISED
WHEN MICHAEL
RETURNED FOR
Halloween II.

Michael 4: The Latest Shape

Don Shanks is a man of few words, which would seem to make him the ideal Shape in *Halloween 5.* "Just because Michael does not say anything doesn't mean playing Michael was not an acting challenge for me," says Shanks. "I may be wearing a mask, but all sorts of things go on inside my head."

The reason for Shanks' getting internal is that the veteran actor/stuntman/director, through the luck of plot development, was handed the most multifaceted Michael Myers to date.

"This Michael is definitely the most animated of the series," says Shanks, who lists the movies *The Life and Times of Grizzly Adams* and the controversial *Silent Night, Deadly Night* on his résumé. "It's not just the physical side of Michael. There's definitely a character with personality, and he gets to show it, especially in the scenes with the little girl. There are one or two tender moments in *Halloween 5* and because of that, I found myself having to go back and forth emotionally. The scene where Michael takes off his mask and sheds a tear was probably the most emotionally charged moment of the film for me. Fortunately, I was out of the mask at the time."

Even beneath the false face, he was doing his fair share of acting. "I've got a background in Greek theater, where a lot of the acting was done in masks," Shanks says. "I also know pantomime, which helps me give a sense of movement to Michael. Even though you get the feeling that Michael does little more than hulk around, I'm really adding some subtle things—or at least trying to."

Shanks calls the not-so-subtle moments on this *Halloween* jaunt "a lot of throwing people through walls and windows. It's definitely a physical film, and Michael gets whacked around quite a bit," states Shanks, who has only seen the original *Halloween* and thus refuses to get specific regarding how he feels his Michael stacks up against those who came before. "I do recognize that people who play the killers in these films tend to develop a certain amount of celebrity status. That's something I think I can deal with. I'm still recognized for *Grizzly Adams*, so I guess I can live with having played Michael."

Shanks reports quite a bit of clowning around on the set, but he says that changed at the moment Michael clocked into work. "I was pretty much myself until the moment I put on the mask," he describes. "When the mask went on, I just sort of clicked into the Myers personality. That's when the joking stopped, because when you've got a mask on and a knife in your hand, things just stop being funny."

JASON'S JOURNAL

BY KANE HODDER

Since the first Friday the 13th *sequel, the Jason actors have been purposefully kept in the shadows and hidden underneath their hockey masks by a publicity-shy studio. Mostly stuntmen, the Voorhees thespians faded back into relative obscurity following their* body count and box-office tallies. *Unlike the monster-actor associations of the past* (Boris Karloff's Frankenstein Monster, Bela Lugosi's Dracula, *etc.) and even the present* (Robert Englund's Freddy Krueger), *no actor has yet claimed Jason as his own, mostly because no one has played him twice. Until Kane Hodder. With the release of* Friday the 13th Part VIII: Jason Takes Manhattan, *actor/stuntman Kane Hodder returned as the master of slaughter. Now, Kane Hodder is Jason.*

As all Crystal Lake historians recall, Hodder first portrayed Jason in 1988's Friday the 13th Part VII: The New Blood. *John Buechler, the film's director, had met Hodder on the above-average Empire productions* Prison *and* Ghost Town, *in which Hodder supplied stunts. Hodder's acting skills were also evident in both films; in* Prison, *he plays the vengeful spirit of a wrongly executed man, and in* Ghost Town, *he's a henchman of lead nasty Devlin. Impressed with his work, Buechler hired the 6-foot-3-inch Hodder in an effort to give the character a frightening new presence and personality.*

Prior to Jason Takes Manhattan, *Hodder coordinated stunts on the Sean Cunningham productions* DeepStar Six *and* The Horror Show. *Filming commenced on the seven-and-a-half-week* Friday the 13th Part VIII *shoot on March 13, 1989 in Vancouver, British Columbia and wrapped on May 4 in Manhattan's Times Square. Additional splatter pickup shots were completed in Los Angeles in mid-June.*

KANE HODDER TRIED ON A NEW LOOK WHEN HE ENCORED AS JASON FOR *Friday the 13th Part VIII.*

As the story of Friday the 13th Part VIII *opens, the graduating class of Crystal Lake High School (if you can believe there are any students left!) embark on an evening cruise to Manhattan. The trouble starts when Rennie (Jensen Daggett) begins having hallucinations of a drowning boy. Pretty soon, a stowaway named Jason drops by to ruin the graduation festivities. Rennie and main squeeze Sean (Scott Reeves) escape the doomed ship in a lifeboat, landing at a lower Manhattan dock. Jason follows the survivors, and proceeds to take a bloody bite out of the Big Apple.*

Hodder kept a location diary during the making of the eighth Friday the 13th *and decided to share portions of it with the fans.*

Friday, April 21 (Day 28)
Location: subway and alley

The most enjoyable day of shooting so far. We start with the alley scenes. My first scene of the night consists of crashing through some boxes and garbage cans, interrupting Scott and Jensen's tender reunion. During the shot's rehearsal, I didn't actually kick any cans or raise a ruckus, because it wasn't necessary. So when we shot it, I ended up scaring the hell out of my poor co-stars, who were not expecting Jason's noisy entrance. These authentic moments of surprise will hopefully make audiences jump out of their skins, too.

When I made *Part VII*, I didn't encounter that many fans on the set by virtue of being out in the middle of the Alabama woods. Not so in downtown Vancouver. Tonight, people are lining the streets at both ends of the alley and surrounding the subway station entrance. Cars stop, while onlookers see me standing here and start hitting each other, yelling, ''Jason!'' (even in the middle of a shot). I sign almost as many autographs as I did at the last Fango convention. I wear the hockey mask at all times to add to Jason's mystique.

Just before lunch, we have to get the shot where Jensen and Scott run into the subway entrance and open the glass doors. Likewise, I enter through those same doors, but without opening them. This is a first for me; I literally crash through a real glass door. I hope it looks as good on the screen as it felt.

At lunch, the director, Rob Hedden, tells me that he really likes what

TOP
JUST ONE OF THE MASKED KILLER'S LENGTHY *Part VIII* **BODY COUNT.**

BOTTOM
JASON TOOK MANHATTAN FOR ONLY A FEW MINUTES; MOST OF THIS SLAUGHTER SEQUEL WAS SHOT IN CANADA.

All Friday the 13th photos © Paramount

we are doing. I hope I am lucky enough to continue working with directors such as Rob Hedden and John Buechler. After chow, we move to the interior of the subway station and onto the train itself. We do a shot where I'm chasing Jensen and Scott through the crowded moving subway car. In an attempt to get away, the heroes pull the emergency cord to suddenly stop the train. The conductor hits the brakes and I go flying backwards. Being totally covered with slime, when I hit the floor I slide about 15 feet down the car. I'm told it looks great.

Next up: a shot where I'm walking through the train. One of the extras sticks his head out in the aisle to glance at Jensen and Scott running by. Well, I'm coming up behind him and his head is still in the way. We all know that Jason wouldn't avoid hitting someone, right? Right, so I club this guy's noggin with my arm as I stomp by. Afterwards, the fellow admits he had done it on purpose in order to stand out from the other extras. Clever dude, huh?

On a break, I return to my trailer, and a cop asks me if we could pose for a picture together. Wait till he develops his film—I did that rabbit ear thing behind his head as a joke. Who says Jason doesn't have a sense of humor?

The night's final scene consists of me coming down the escalator and ramming into people. The last person I get to is the 1st AD [assistant director] on the show, so I grab his face with a handful of slime and slam him backwards. He's a good sport about it. We wrap at dawn.

Wednesday, April 26
(Day 31)
Location: studio sewer set

We fly to New York next week to shoot in Times Square. I can't wait. I truly enjoy playing this character. Anybody who remembers the fact that I once put live worms in my mouth for a scene in *Prison* would not be surprised

at today's fun. The shot calls for water to come gushing out of my mouth. Well, ever since I was a little kid, I've had the ability to vomit fluids on cue! Consequently, I drank two full pitchers of water, and when the scene comes on the screen, you will know that it is not a special effect. It's real.

Later, a drenching of another sort transpires. In this scene a flood comes rushing down the sewer and crashes into me. Martin Becker, the special FX guy, built a terrific system for dumping water into the set. We complete the stunt twice. The second time, however, knocks the wind out of me. Over 2,000 gallons slam into me in one gush from 6 feet away. As the water topples me over, my leg gets caught in a pipe and for a second I think, "Uh-oh." But I breathlessly manage to slip away and the whole stunt works perfectly. At the end of the night I have to go to the bathroom and vomit again because of all the water still left in my stomach. I hope it was worth it. Wrap at midnight.

Friday, April 28 (Day 33)
Location: studio sewer set

Last day of shooting in Vancouver before we fly to New York. We do the water-dump stunt again to make sure we have the coverage we need. This time, Marty heats the water to make it more comfortable. It's like getting blasted by a maniacal jacuzzi! At dinner break, Rob gives the entire cast and crew *F-13 Part VIII* sweatshirts. Pretty nice gesture.

The last shot of the night consists of Jensen's character hitting me in the face with a bucket of slime. Since Jensen isn't needed in the shot, the 1st AD is commissioned to throw the crap at me from off-camera. He misses, so he passes the bucket to Rob for Take Two. Rob's attempt is off the mark as well, and a big wad of slime just grazes my hockey mask and splatters on the wall behind me. Take Three! Rob's second try is similar to his first, and once again, he nails that pesky wall. OK. Take Four.

Rob is psyched! Wham! Direct hit in the kisser! Brightly-colored green slime slowly drips off the mask. Yeah! We wrap at 7:30 a.m.

By the time I get back to the hotel, it is 8:30 a.m. Saturday. My face is still green from the slime, my hair is matted, I have makeup on and I've been up all night working. I arrive at the hotel and sneak through the back doors of the restaurant area to avoid talking to anyone; I'm tired and I need a shower. Badly. When I walk through the doors, I end up right in the middle of a Women's Club breakfast function! I'm shocked. I stop and realize that everyone in the room is staring at me, dumbstruck. Fortunately, the hostess immediately explains who I am and the reason for my sorry shape. The ladies breathe a sigh of relief. In fact, I get some autographed picture requests from several of those very same women.

That's it! We are finished shooting in Vancouver.

Look out New York, here comes Jason!

**TOP RIGHT
A CENSORED SCENE
FROM JASON'S
KILLER CRUISE.**

PINHEAD'S PROGRESS

BY DOUG BRADLEY

Those of you who attended FANGORIA's Los Angeles *Weekend of Horrors* in April 1989 heard me confidently state, *"Hellraiser III* is imminent." This was no lie; I had been told we would start that autumn. And if you were in Boston in the summer of 1990, or New York in January 1991, you would have heard me say exactly the same thing (a bit less confidently). By the time I got to Dearborn in July of '91, the song remained the same, although now I was singing with full orchestral backing. The false starts, the blocks and delays (which as a mere actor I was, of course, powerless to influence) had suddenly disappeared. I had signed on the dotted line, and everything was set to roll at Atlantic Studios in High Point, North Carolina in September '91. Shortly before I left England, Tony Timpone called me and asked if I would keep a diary during filming for publication. So here it is—a slice of life on and off the set as I don the nails and latex to play Pinhead for the third time in *Hellraiser III: Hell on Earth.*

Monday, September 23:

After three and a half years of waiting, the day has finally dawned: At 7:00 this morning, the cameras finally rolled on *Hellraiser III: Hell on Earth*, although for me the action does not begin until Thursday. I flew in from London yesterday, and right now I'm easing off the jet-lag under cloudless Carolina skies, alternately dipping into the script and the pool. Pete Atkins has written a powerful screenplay and if all goes well, I'm confident that this will prove a more-than-worthy successor to the first two films.

Appropriately, my first few days will be taken up with the reincarnation of Pin-

All Pinhead photos © Dimension

head, released from the torture pillar where we last saw him at the end of *Hellbound*. Although I know this character well by now—having talked and answered so many questions about him over the last few years—I am feeling distinctly nervous about approaching him again. How do I keep him fresh, keep him interesting? How do I live up to other people's expectations? Basically, *can I still do it?* The reassuring thing is that this is a subtly different Pinhead. Freed of his human soul and the constraints of the box, he is a darker, more sinister and glibly malevolent vision, which has sparked my imagination afresh.

I make my way to the set this morning (all of two minutes' walk from my hotel room) to watch this act of collective insanity we call filmmaking get underway. No going back now, I think: It's a one-way ticket to whatever fate has in store.

Thursday, September 26:

And so it begins! My first day back as Pinhead. It feels so strange to sit down among the familiar faces of Bob Keen's FX crew and watch the makeup spread across my face again. Paul Jones, who was an assistant on the Lylesburg makeup for *Nightbreed*, is in charge of the process this time around, and Steve Painter, who worked on the Pinhead makeup for *Hellbound*, is assisting him. The latex has been redesigned to go on in just two pieces and cut the application time down, and it works perfectly. The three and a half years (and my paranoia) simply melt away. I only have to reach out and there he is, smiling darkly, embracing me and carrying me away with him!

A familiar frisson runs around the set as, nerves a-jangle, I walk on. So many people come to catch a glimpse that I have to ask Paul Martin, our AD, to request that they leave, as I start to feel more like a freak in a sideshow than the all-confident Pope of Hell! My first shots require me to stand inside the torture pillar with only my face revealed as the resurrection process begins. A curious moment: As we ease my head through the hole in the pillar, two pins are dislodged, but when we try to replace them, there's only a place for one. The fantasy bleeds into reality. . .

An unexpected bonus awaits me: I am extremely nearsighted, and the combination of this and Pinhead's dark contact lenses has meant that up to now, I've spent my time on set in a myopic twilight. To my delight, the new lenses have been made to my prescription. Miracle of miracles, I can see! Only another nearsighted actor can appreciate what it means to be able to focus on all quarters of the acting area and, most importantly, my fellow actors. Or one actor in this case, as I'm working opposite the excellent Kevin Bernhardt, who plays J.P., a nightclub owner who purchases the torture pillar from an art gallery unaware of the secrets this little masterpiece contains.

Acting inside such a confined space, completely immobile and with my back and neck contorted to hold my head rigid against the pillar, is tough. Not being able to move around between takes to dissipate/maintain energy is especially frustrating. When the inevitable note comes from Tony Hickox—"We have to believe you're physically part of this pillar, not an actor with his head stuck through a hole"—we both break up laughing. Tony is the third director I've now worked with as Pinhead, and we've hardly spoken before this first meeting on set. Later, he tells me how weird he found it trying to give directions to a disembodied head! On a more serious note, I make it clear to him that, while this is my third outing as the character, I consider this to be a new beginning in many ways and want his input as much as possible. In fact, our working relationship is instantly good.

Wrapping at about 8 p.m., I head back to the FX trailer feeling more satisfied than with any day's work as Pinhead so far. As the makeup starts to come off, Bob

Keen appears with a couple of bottles of champagne to celebrate my "25th birthday" —my 25th day in the Pinhead latex. Producers Larry Mortorff and Olive McQueen, unit publicist Steve Jones and Tony join us as we toast Pinhead's return.

Saturday, September 28:

Not called until 11 a.m., I wake at 5, phone my wife Lynne and 2-year-old son Robert back in England, and then sleep on until 9. Later, on set, we continue to work on Pinhead's reincarnation, which means another day trapped inside the pillar. God, it'll be good to get out of there. With only an immobile head to act with, everything seems terribly false, the more so since most of my work is reaction as my new recruit J.P. battles to feed me my second victim, Terri (played by Paula Marshall).

When the main unit wraps at 7:30, I continue to work with Bob Keen on 2nd-unit scenes. As the evening wears on, I start to get that familiar feeling of constriction, as though the makeup is tightening around my head, and I can start to feel the individual pins bouncing against my skin when I walk.

We pass the time between shots trying to see how many movie titles we can get the word "pin" into: *Towering Pinferno*, *The Pins of Navarone*, *Twelve Angry Pins*, *Gone With the Pins*, *The Third Pin*, *The Day the Pins Stood Still*, *Seven Deadly Pins*, etc. Oh, and not forgetting of course *Pinocchio*!

Dr. Bill Walker, a local optometrist, is on set with me to take care of the lenses. When we wrap, he examines my eyes with fluorescent dye and tells me he can see irritation in them. We're going to have to take care; there's a long way to go yet.

Sunday, September 29:

Visited the High Point Gun Show today. A crash course in culture shock for me: guns by the hundred, folks strolling with automatic weapons slung across their shoulders. The fact that I could have walked away from the show with a shotgun and enough ammunition to shoot up the town bothers my delicate English sensibilities, to the amusement of my American colleagues.

Monday, September 30:

The first shot today is of Pinhead, back in full regalia, as he finally breaks free of the pillar. Then it's back to the trailer to return the makeup to pillar state, a time-consuming process. We then carry on, filling in the details of Pinhead's seduction of his first victims.

At the end of a long, hard day, Tony and I pull a quick gag. J.P., finally won over, approaches Pinhead in the pillar and asks, "How do we start?" Pinhead's reply is, "It has already begun," but after doing my best impersonation of a Method actor, I answer in a high-pitched Northern English accent, "Don't ask me, you daft bastard, I'm only a pillar." And it's a wrap!

Tuesday, October 1:

As I prepare to leave my hotel room for a midday shoot, I get a call from the production office. They've decided to try again on the contact lenses, so I'm driven out to Dr. Walker's office in Ashboro for an eye test. I will be able to wear the new lenses all day, which will make life easier for all concerned.

The delayed start means I'm not in full makeup until nearly 6 p.m. for the 2ndunit work. After shooting some promo/publicity material, we toil away, working around Pinhead's rebirth and the deaths of his victims. This requires another lengthy makeup change midway through the evening, removing all the pins and repainting. It's a long night's work before I'm finally free of latex by 3 a.m., but assuming no reshoots are necessary, I can kiss goodbye to acting inside the pillar—and that's a great relief.

Thursday, October 3:

Pinhead's first-ever day on location. We head off to Market Square in High Point for the scene in which the reincarnated Pinhead blasts his way out of J.P.'s room into the nightclub, scattering partygoers before him. As they try to escape, all the exit doors slam shut and "No one here gets out alive." The set is filled with locally recruited extras, and it's a strange feeling as I walk out. The set falls completely silent as they step back and simply stare at me. After a long, hot day, they're working really hard, and their simulated panic and confusion is totally convincing.

Wrapping at midnight, I mingle among the extras, then slip out of costume, pull jeans and a jacket over my leotard and join them in the upstairs bar for a couple of beers—still in makeup. The well-dressed Cenobite out on the town! Signing autographs, having my picture taken, Slade pounding away in the background—it's like a spaced-out Fango convention! I even get two upfront requests from girls to father their children—as Pinhead (note: I declined).

Saturday, October 5:

Back to Market Square for my first scene with Terry Farrell, who plays the lead role of Joey Summerskill, a TV news reporter who finds herself caught up in Pinhead's resurrection. Here, she returns to the nightclub to find herself trapped in the aftermath of Pinhead's unpitying slaughter—thousands massacred on a whim. And what a setup! It's like a Cabaret of Death. She is lured into a room to find herself center-stage with an audience of corpses, neatly seated in rows. And facing her is one of Pinhead's creations, Diceman, standing in a wooden frame with barbed wire wrapped around his head and dice for eyeballs. It's powerful stuff, and for me the effect is enhanced by my new lenses, which have a strong red tint. The whole reality appears to have been drenched in blood.

The chemistry between Terry and myself is instantly good, and this first confrontation between the story's two central characters goes as well as I could have hoped. It feels as though everyone is caught up in the atmosphere—and if it's as powerful on celluloid as it felt in reality, it's going to be a memorable moment.

Tuesday–Wednesday, October 8–9:

Two back-to-back night shoots on a building site at Wake Forest University in Winston-Salem. Although the daytime temperatures are up in the 70s, it has suddenly turned bitterly cold at night—below 40 on Tuesday. It's odd to see people I've only seen in shorts, T-shirts and shades suddenly decked out in hats, scarves, gloves and winter coats.

We've jumped to the climax of the movie as Joey—with the puzzle box—is cornered by Pinhead and his new Cenobites. His intention is to destroy the Lament Configuration and thus remove the possibility of being returned to his former existence. Hell, he's having fun out here—who wants to go home now? His army are not true Cenobites, not made in hell, but hand-crafted by Pinhead. Tuesday is not a good night for me: In the makeup chair at 8:30 p.m., I don't get on set until 5 a.m. for two quick shots, and then I'm wrapped. All in a night's work, I know, but carrying this makeup around is hard work at the best of times and being left in it all night can drive a man insane. I'm not a happy camper, but a blood-red sunrise on the drive back to the hotel lifts my spirits.

Wednesday more than makes up for it, though. Not only is it about 10 degrees warmer, but I feel as though I've put in a worthwhile night's work by the end of it. The FX trailer is positively awash with Cenobites. There's Kevin (J.P.), pistons smashing through his skull; Paula Marshall (Terri), a nightmare of sex and cigarettes; Ken Carpenter (Doc, Joey's cameraman), camera lens zooming in and out of one eye socket; Eric (the nightclub DJ), CD player sunk into his chest, discs buried in his head; and Rick the barman, a study in barbed wire. The last-named is being played by Pete Atkins, and it's a great, perverse kick for me to watch him get the Cenobite treatment—and oh, is he enjoying it!

On campus, word is out that we're here. Groups of students have gathered to watch, cheering and applauding as we leave the FX trailer and pounding on the sides of the bus as we drive to the set, shouting, "Pinhead! Pinhead! You're the man!" We let them on set in small groups to get a closer look.

Napoleon-like, Pinhead stands aloof on a raised bank of mud, watching his troops advance on the apparently helpless Joey. Needless to say, things don't go quite as planned—they never do, do they? (Note for future scripts—ain't it time he stopped being such a loser?!) Phil Nutman is down to do a set report for Fango and, perched precariously among the mud and iron girders, drinking coffee through a straw (me, not Phil), we grab a quick interview. Amazingly, when we wrap at 4:30 a.m., there's still a little knot of fans gathered at the entrance to the set.

Friday, October 11:

A brief night for me, as I make my first appearance as the army officer from *Hellbound*, now christened Captain Elliott Spenser. I work with the 2nd unit for the scene where Joey, watching Kirsty Cotton recount her story on video at the Channard Institute, is suddenly confronted by Elliott's ghostly image breaking through and speaking directly to her. This done, I go over to watch events on the street location in Greensboro. Which one? Would you believe—Elm Street? A Pinhead on Elm Street. Believe it!

In the early hours, Kevin Bernhardt is wrapped and finished with his part of the film. Hugs and kisses all around. Oh, I hate this business of suddenly saying goodbye to people you're just getting to know. I've gotten on well with Kevin, and I'm sad to see him go.

There follows quite a lull in my schedule, as several nights are spent shooting the chaos on the street that greets Joey as she flees from Pinhead in the nightclub. Ray Bivens' FX crew is having fun; bringing down power lines, exploding shop fronts, blowing up fire hydrants, etc. I work with the 2nd unit on Thursday the 17th, briefly establishing the scene where Pinhead follows Joey through the mayhem he's orchestrating for her. Great excitement for me earlier in the week as I make my debut as a makeup artist. Bob, stretched for spare hands, needs a hole-in-the-head makeup inflicted on a bystander by the Doc Cenobite—and I volunteer. Luckily, Steve Painter is playing the part, so he talks me through it. Chasing around on set, touching up, applying blood, cleaning up between takes—jeez, this is hard work. Think I'll stick to acting! Just before dawn on Friday, Ray gives a grand finale to Greensboro by blowing up two police cars.

Saturday, October 19:

Back on the stage at High Point, it's a positively schizophrenic night for me as we shoot the climactic confrontation between Pinhead and Elliott, starting out in human form and switching to Cenobite at about 2 a.m. It's weird enough stepping onto Steve Hardie's recreation of the Quonset hut from *Hellbound*—complete with the same radio we used at Pinewood, which he managed to dig out of the prophouse in London—but I'm completely tripped out by the sight of Pinhead standing there, waiting for me. Kevin, my stand-in, has won the nomination to double Pinhead. I point out that he's the only other person ever to have worn the full Pinhead makeup and costume and that thousands of fans—the entire Fango readership for a start—would pay a lot of money to do what he's doing. I suddenly realize just how jealously protective of the character I've become. It is deeply unsettling to me to see Pinhead disembodied, as it were—I just don't like it! It all catches up with me when Tony suggests I demonstrate to Kevin what Pinhead's reaction to a specific moment should be. Having considered that, I step back into Elliott's marks, the camera rolls, and I deliver Elliott's line in Pinhead's voice. CUT!

Sunday, October 20:

Two weeks of night shoots come to an end as Elliott and Joey meet on Flanders Field, amid the carnage of WWI. Steve Hardie has worked miracles again, creating an astoundingly real and atmospheric battlefield out of a local garbage landfill.

I have to say that it's a great relief and liberation to be doing walking, talking human-being acting. And only five minutes in the makeup chair! Terry Farrell is so easy to work with. Once again the chemistry between us is good, and despite the cold, a superb night's work is really done and I'm back in bed before the sun is up.

The memory of this night's filming will live with me for a long time. One moment is particularly memorable. As Terry and I head back to the trailer to get warm while the next setup is lit, I look back and see a little group of extras in battle-dress. They've gathered at the edge of a mortar crater around one of the FX fires and are

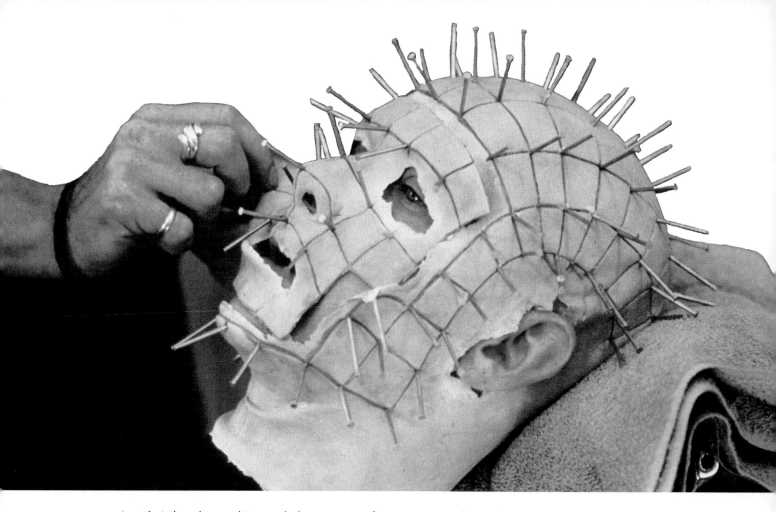

warming their hands, smoking and chatting. Just for a moment, this is the real thing. This sense of a tangible reality seems to spread to everybody: I hear several people comment that this is the kind of thing you just don't see in the average horror flick. That, I hope, will prove to be one of the strengths of this movie. But after all, if anything qualified for the tag *Hell on Earth*, the trenches of the First World War were surely it.

BRADLEY UNDERGOES THE LENGTHY PIN PLACEMENT PROCESS.

Tuesday, October 22:

From Flanders to another glimpse of Hell on Earth—Vietnam, and Joey's dreams of searching for the father she never knew. It's another first for me—Pinhead in broad daylight, manipulating Joey's fantasy to win back the box and destroy it and her. Vietnam is a N.C. beanfield! By the end of the day, it's a mad scramble to get the shots in before the sun drops behind the trees. Suddenly, this really feels like low-budget moviemaking! To add to the indignity, I have to tape Pinhead's skirts up around my knees in order to pursue Terry across the uneven ground without falling on my face.

Thursday–Friday, October 24–25:

My two toughest days so far—32 hours in total—as we reach what for me is the apotheosis of Pinhead over all three films and move right into the heart of Christian theology. Pursuing Joey from the nightclub and through the streets, Pinhead finally corners her in the church in which she has taken refuge. Confronted by a priest, Pinhead simply melts the crucifix he holds out for protection and calmly steps up to the altar. Removing two pins from his head, he drives them through the palms of his hands in a mockery of the crucifixion. As I adopt the pose and utter the words, "I am the way," Ray Bivens' FX crew blow up the big stained glass window behind me and send huge flames up behind it. With earplugs driven as deep into my ears as I can manage, I get through that without flinching—but I'm not so lucky with the next shot.

As I stare down at Joey and the priest, the altar collapses in front of me. That's fine, but the dais I'm standing on lurches backwards and for a moment, it feels as though the whole thing is going to collapse under me before it jolts back to its original position. I'm OK, but I know that a distinct look of alarm has spread across the supposedly inscrutable features of Pinhead and that I've taken a few wobbly steps backwards to keep my balance. It'll take some fast cutting to work around that one!

Pinhead's next act is to force-feed his own flesh, plucked from the wounds on his chest, to the priest in a grotesque mockery of the Last Supper: "This is *my* body. This is *my* blood." It's powerful, powerful stuff, and I'm incredibly energized by the atmosphere of it. Pinhead takes none of this seriously, of course—it's just fun and games to him. I just have a nagging worry about how much of it will survive intact. It will upset and shock people, which as far as I'm concerned, is as it should be. We shall see. . .

Saturday, October 26:

Back into human guise to continue the scene which begins and ends on Flanders Field: Elliott explaining to Joey just who and what she is up against. Elliott's ghost takes her on a brief time trip: From Flanders we step into a street bazaar in India, with a frozen tableau of me purchasing the box; then into the Quonset hut with my dummy in the act of solving the puzzle (again, a frozen image around which Terry and I walk and talk); from there to the "torture room" of the first two films; then back to Flanders.

We finish this scene in the Quonset hut. It's only one shot, but Tony has set up an extremely complex camera move, and it takes forever to get it running smoothly. And when we do, the inevitable happens—I miss my mark, Terry loses her line in sight of home base. It's 20 takes before we're done, and it's a 1st-unit wrap for me.

To celebrate, I've arranged wrap champagne for everyone. We're also celebrating AD Paul Martin's birthday and the engagement of Steve Painter of Bob Keen's crew to Hilary Momberger, our script supervisor. After the bubbly, we decamp to The Boiler Room at Market Square for a party which lasts well into Sunday. I spend the final week of the shoot working with the 2nd unit.

Wednesday, October 30:

I've spent three days working on various stages of the merging of Pinhead and Elliott, and suddenly that's it! I'm wrapped! Three and a half years of waiting, and it's all over in six short weeks. As there are only two days of filming left and the wrap party is on Saturday, I've decided not to fly home immediately. On Halloween evening, I sit in the hotel bar with Paul Jones and watch the last half hour of *Bride of Frankenstein* on TV. Next door, a Christian revivalist meeting is in full, noisy swing; a few hundred yards away, *Hellraiser III* is in its final stages. Across America, ghosts and vampires, Freddys and Jasons (and perhaps one or two Pinheads) trick-or-treat their way through the streets. And that seems like a good image on which to fade to black.

I'm quietly confident that I've done my best work ever in the last month and a half—I hope I'll still feel that way when I sit down to watch the finished film. I've been helped along the way by a magnificent cast and crew who've worked hard and played hard: I will leave many friends when I fly back to London on Monday.

This may have been Hell on Earth, but it's been Heaven in North Carolina.

INDEX